The Resources of Kind

Genre-Theory in the Renaissance

UNA'S LECTURES

Una's Lectures, delivered annually on the Berkeley campus, memorialize Una Smith, who received her B.S. in History from Berkeley in 1911 and her M.A. in 1913. They express her esteem for the humanities in enlarging the scope of the individual mind. When appropriate, books deriving from the Una's lectureship are published by the University of California Press:

1. *The Resources of Kind: Genre-Theory in the Renaissance,* by Rosalie L. Colie. 1973

ROSALIE L. COLIE

The Resources of Kind
Genre-Theory in the Renaissance

Edited by Barbara K. Lewalski

UNIVERSITY OF CALIFORNIA PRESS

Berkeley • Los Angeles • London

University of California Press
Berkeley and Los Angeles, California
University of California Press, Ltd.
London, England
Copyright © 1973, by
The Regents of the University of California
ISBN: 0–520–02397–8
Library of Congress Catalog Card Number: 72–95307
Printed in the United States of America

Contents

Foreword

Rosalie Littell Colie delivered the four lectures which comprise this volume in the annual "Una's Lectures in the Humanities" series at the University of California at Berkeley, in May 1972. Her plan was to revise and augment them considerably and to annotate them fully before publication, turning them into a comprehensive and richly documented study of the theory and uses of genre in the Renaissance. On July 7, 1972, she died suddenly in a boating accident.

In their present format, then, these lectures do not represent Rosalie Colie's final intention as regards her investigation of Renaissance genre. But they are in themselves a contribution of the first order of importance to literary history and critical theory—enriched by prodigious learning lightly worn, by brilliant new perspectives and insights, by wideranging speculation, by elegance of language. The significance of these essays lies especially in their emphasis upon the rich variousness of genres and generic functions in Renaissance literature, dispelling all basis for the modern prejudice that genre is some kind of straightjacket, stifling originality. Miss Colie persuades her audience to acknowledge their constant and inevitable dependence upon genre (kind) for any apprehension of reality in life as in literature, and then displays how genre functions as a mode of communication—a set of recognized frames or fixes upon the world. In this perspective genre is not only a matter of literary convention, as we sometimes tend to think—a way of signalling the connections between topic and treatment within the literary system—but it is also a myth or metaphor for man's vision of truth.

Fundamental to Rosalie Colie's exploration of genre is her identification of an underlying tension in Renaissance genre theory, producing on the one hand the sharp differentiation of the kinds to produce these different sets on life, and on the other the recognition of literature as a totality, a *paideia* comprehending and transmitting all knowledge even as Homer's *Iliad* was said to have done. The latter conception validated for literary purposes many kinds often excluded by strict constructionists of Aristotle or Horace, and also permitted mixtures, transformations, and amalgamations of kinds. Within this framework, the lectures touch upon an amazing variety of topics: the emergence of the smallest kinds (adage, epigram, emblem, sonnet) and the assimilation of their conventions into larger forms; the proliferation and elevation to literary respectability of many kinds often excised from the literary canon—histories, philosophical poems, prose fiction (*Gargantua and Pantagruel*), dialogues, debates, archaeological treatises (Thomas Browne's *Urne-Buriall*); the deliberate creation of new forms—*nova reperta* in the arts to match those new stars found in the heavens—such as the essay, the picaresque novel, the modern historical "epic" (D'Aubigne's *Les Tragiques*). Finally the study suggests that the greatness of such works as *Paradise Lost* and *King Lear* derives in large part from their being encyclopedic works of "mixed genre" which incorporate and juxtapose virtually the entire range of generic conventions, displaying through these different "fixes" on experience the full range of human possibilities.

In editing these lectures I have made no substantive changes or additions, and few stylistic ones, though I have in several places supplied more complete references to books and authors. Also, I have chosen from among the large number of

emblems mentioned or alluded to in the text of Chapter II
a selection which I hope may fairly illustrate the points made
in that chapter. Though we must regret that we cannot have
the book Rosalie Colie would have made from these essays,
it is fitting in some ways that her final contribution to Renaissance studies—already so greatly in her debt for seminal
books and articles on Constantine Huygens, the Cambridge
Platonists and the Dutch Arminians, Renaissance paradoxy,
Andrew Marvell, Shakespeare, Donne, Herbert, Milton, and
much more—should be a set of lectures now given the perma-
nence of print. For this format perhaps best displays her
special style of scholarly discourse—the wide-ranging but dis-
ciplined intellectual speculation and the constant concern
with scholarly method and process, which are in some respects
her most enduring contributions to the students and col-
leagues fortunate enough to have worked with her.

Barbara K. Lewalski
Brown University

I
Genre-Systems and the Functions of Literature

In a period like our own, in which forms seem generally restrictions—the fetters from which we are dutybound to escape, or brands of an unimaginative establishmentarianism, or (at their worst) self-made prisons in which we acquiesce—the protracted discussion of literary form and forms, in a period long past, may seem at best antiquarian and at worst irresponsible. Indeed, even in literary circles, the idea of "kind," of genre, is hardly popular nowadays; the venerable new criticism on which we have all been brought up has notoriously excoriated the idea of genre (Croce, Wimsatt); and the distinguished marriage of its daughter, rhetorical criticism, with linguistic discourse-analysis was not undertaken on the authority of the idea of genre, nor yet of the actual genres writers wrote their texts in. Grander modes of literary criticism either involve closer attention to form than genres seem to demand (i.e., linguistic-structural criticism) or far *less* attention to texts, as in phenomenological or anthropological structuralist criticism. When a recent book relying heavily on new-critical assumptions and lightly bandying many of the techniques of more modern versions of literary criticism calls itself "Beyond Formalism," surely it is reactionary to consider genre (or, as I prefer, its cognate translation, "kind") and genres in Renaissance literature.

I shelter behind the title of these lectures, which were designed to permit speculation and to conjoin disciplines that are not always comfortable bedfellows; for I think that, as an expression of Renaissance culture relevant to more than its belletristic production, the notion of genre is historically significant. More than that, I think it is historically "true"—and, since Una's Gift to her blundering but idealistic Redcrosse Knight was no less than truth, perhaps I may offer my simplistic essay "Of Truth" under her protection. I cannot of course aspire heroically to truth, as Redcrosse did; my essay is in the occupational, or georgic kind, a short-term definition, a modest proposal, a teacher's attempt at order. By means of genre and genre-systems, I hope to understand something about a profession, a calling, in the long Renaissance, and thereby to understand how literary works were thought to come into being. My enterprise is, then, historical rather than critical, but since I think that a generic theory of literature is fundamentally comparative and therefore, as Thomas Rosenmeyer's book on the eclogue has shown us, fundamentally *critical*, perhaps later in these lectures some of my remarks may aspire to criticism too.

It has gradually dawned on me that one way to understand some of the interconnections of Renaissance literature, a bulk of magnificent writing that somehow seems to belong culturally together, is to tackle notions of literary kind: what kinds of "kind" did writers recognize, and why? Why should there have been such bitter critical battles in sixteenth-century Italy over Dante's *Commedia*, Speroni's un-Sophoclean tragedy *Canace e Macareo*, Ariosto's and Tasso's epics, Guarini's tragicomical play? Since three of these works are self-evidently masterpieces and the other two by no means bad, why weren't critics and readers able to take them gratefully for whatever they were, instead of making them objects of critical inquiry and even disapproval?

Part of the answer lies in the hold that concepts of genre had on writers and their readers in the Renaissance—a period which, for purposes of discussion, I take to begin with Petrarca and to end with Swift. For reasons that may seem familiar to us in one way and with results that seem very odd, literate young men in the Renaissance turned to a cultural ideal which they defined as other and better than their own, very much as alternative life-styles to our own are now sought in Eastern, primitive, or remote cultures. All around us, we see Eastern modes of thought and belief, Eastern arts and crafts: to the anthropologist or the historian lamentably detached from their cultural habitat—but loved as symbols for the virtues attributed to that habitat. With something of the same enthusiasm and the same synchronic selectivism with which other cultural elements are now defined as alternative value-systems to our own, generation after generation of Renaissance young men were willing to turn to antiquity, adapting to their needs and desires those elements in antiquity which they could recognize as useful or symbolically relevant.

It was a book revolution: texts were overwhelmingly the sources from which the new liberation came, although visual sources were also enormously important in stimulating the painting, sculpture and (especially) architecture of the time. The longer we work with ancient texts however, the more obvious it is that word governed visual image, even then. Vitruvius was as important as Roman ruins visible and tangible. The texts in question were recovered from oblivion, published on the new-fangled presses, edited and quarreled over—and endlessly imitated. Why such models, and whence came their peculiar power? To be able to answer that question is to understand the Renaissance, I think: I do not pretend to offer answers to this here, but only to take—as do all the articles in paperbacks called "Six Lectures on Renaissance Thought," "The Renaissance: Aspects of its Culture," etc.—

this glorification of ancient culture as a given. Certainly, in literature it *was* a given: from the fifteenth century on, those interested in the new learning (that is, the old learning restored) insisted on imitating; they made models of classical texts, chiefly Cicero, translated and imitated them. Rhetorical education, always a model-following enterprise, increasingly stressed *structures* as well as styles to be imitated in the humane letters—epistles, orations, discourses, dialogues, histories, poems—always discoverable to the enthusiastic new man of letters by kind.

Such classification, I think, was rhetorically based, but it tended toward a new kind, *poetics*, a kind which, when Aldus published the text of Aristotle's *Poetics*, did not yet exist; that epoch-making discourse appeared in a volume called "Ancient Rhetoricians." In one generation, however, Aristotle's *Poetics*, together with Horace's long-known *ars poetica*, the epistle to the Pisos, had established a Renaissance genre, on which this study fundamentally relies. I shall refer from time to time to some of the many *artes poeticae* written in the period, since from them we can recover the ideas consciously held, governing the written criticism and theory of the Renaissance. From "real" literature as opposed to criticism and theory, of course, we recover what is far more important, the *unwritten* poetics by which writers worked and which they themselves created.

At this point you may be saying: but is she suggesting that literary kinds, genres, are peculiar to ancient literature and Renaissance literature? What is *The Canterbury Tales* but a magnificent repertory of medieval narrative kinds? Were not poetic forms highly developed in the Provençal and Spanish schools of the twelfth and thirteenth centuries, and in the chambers of rhetoric of the late Middle Ages? Of course: and there are always kinds, forms, schemata, in all the arts, even now, when we flee from them that sometime did them seek. (If a Campbell's soup tin, then, obviously, a Brillo box.) In the last fifty years, we have learnt a good deal about our perceptions of anything at all, notably, that these perceptions are mediated by forms, collections, collocations, associations; we have learnt, even, that we learn so naturally by forms and formulae that we often entirely fail to recognize them for what they are.

In arts other than literature, there is far less hostility to the notion of generic schemata than still prevails in literary study. To turn for a moment to the topic of last year's Una's Lectures, architecture, we expect genres there. We recognize without difficulty a cottage, a house, a *palazzo*, and know how they differ from each other. If, like me, we have recently moved house, then we may have discovered those charming domestic subgenres, "Garrison Colonial" and "Raised Ranch House," both now common in ancient New England villages. On campuses, of whatever mixed style they may be, we can usually tell the administration building from all the others. In the East, at least, prisons are unmistakable still. Though modern schools are too light for prison-house shade, it is only their window-space that distinguishes them from modern factories. When I was a child, banks spoke darkly, in metaphor: they used to look like the Palazzo Medici-Riccardi, oblong buildings of dark stone rusticated below, with beautiful neoclassical windows covered with half a cage. Some eclectic banks also had Strozzi lamps outside. Now banks speak a different language: the dark defensive fortresses where money was secure have turned into glass cubes where all the money-changers, from tellers to first vice-presidents, perform their tasks openly, transparently, before the public eye. Perhaps the 1929 crash and the 1933 bank failures had as much to do with this alteration in the generic form as new styles in architecture or any change of heart in bankers. The point is, though, that the genre has changed, although its functions remain more or less stable: we shall live, I trust, to see whether the adobe defensive house of the Bank of America in Isla Vista, with sprinklers built into the architectural decoration, becomes the subgeneric bank for campuses of the University of California, or any university where students see in the bank the source of all their woe.

Function tells loudly in architecture, dominating, in most cases, our idea of what we see. Though its critics likened the Guggenheim Museum when new to the old Wanamaker's and to a parking garage, I never heard of anyone's trying to buy soap or to park his car there: for all its *art nouveau* radicalism, Mr. Wright's building advertises itself as just what it is— hanging space. Sometimes the genres are less clearly defined: my nearsightedness is responsible for my shouting "There!" on the highway, only to be told that the Howard Johnson's oasis I indicate is really a Lutheran Church. It is the steeple-cupola that muddles me: a symbolic barn cupola with weather-vane, to show how very olde-timey Howard Johnson's pre-packed food is; an unstressed steeple for the ecumenical building anxious to seem not so very different from weekday buildings. Culture alters genre, to bring some of them quite close together—nonetheless, even though churches may have church-suppers and weddings be held at Howard Johnson's, we cannot really confuse them for long.

Music is even more dependent than architecture upon formal genre and the notion of form. Dudley North knew this when he wrote in his *Forest of Varieties*, "Musick hath its Anthems, Pavens, Fantesies, Galliards, Courantoes, Ayres, Sarabands, Toyes, Cromatiques, etc. And Verses have their Hymns, Tragedies, Satyres, Heroiques, Sonets, Odes, Songs, Epigrams, Distiques, and Strong Lines, which are their Cromatiques." Even literary critics accept as *données* such formal divisions in music: that they have altered from North's list into other names—tone-poems, symphonies, concerti, etc.— only shows the more readily how automatically we accept the

6

generic conventions in music. We owe a great deal also to formal patterns of allusion in the various musical genres: "*alla turca*" may not convince a dedicated ethnomusicologist of its authenticity, but it serves to remind us of an historical continuum when oriental and occidental cultures shared a long European border. "Contradans" may owe very little to English folk-dances, but it speaks to sophisticated eighteenth-century concepts of what that form ought to have been. A musical "Passion" is radically different from a Mass, and we rarely complain of formal rigidity in either. We recognize at once why one symphony is called "Pastorale" and another "Eroica," even why a French verbal form designates the one, and an Italian the other, without perhaps realizing the literary origins of this suggestiveness; we accept furthermore that both are members of the same class, although their adjectives would seem to deny it, with the cuckoo of one and the trumpets of the other calling up opposed sets of association.

It is much as musical forms mean to us that literary forms "meant" to Renaissance writers—a genre was, in Claudio Guillén's nice phrase, "a challenge to match an imaginative structure to reality." With that last word I have introduced the shibboleth and stumblingblock of Renaissance Aristotelianism, the idea of mimesis, or the imitation of *reality*. It was in the service of this mimesis that Aristotle contributed a social dimension, or decorum, to the literary modes he canonized, narrative, dramatic, and lyric, modes then subdivided into genres—epic, tragic, comic, etc. In the imitation of reality, a high style befits its high subject—epic or tragic; a low style a low subject, comedy or some lyric forms. Since Cicero expressed outright what is implied in Aristotle's formula, namely that styles must not be mixed (comic style is a defect in tragedy, tragic style in comedy, etc.), we can understand why subscribers to this theory fussed so over Guarini's *Il pastor fido*, which did what Sidney complained of English plays' doing in mingling "Kings and Clownes." The breaking of decorum, in this case, has to do with social as well as with aesthetic premises.

It seems to me that even though the chief concept of mimesis may often have acted as a constraint upon literary innovation in the Renaissance, another version of imitation, simply the imitation of formal models, was in spite of its inbuilt conservatism a factor for literary change and imaginative experiment. Further, though I insist that there were concepts of kind which *did* govern imitation in both senses, there were many more kinds than were recognized in official literary philosophy; and it is by these competing notions of kind that the richness and variety of Renaissance letters were assured.

By looking at Renaissance notions of genre and generic system, I hope to convey also some of the social importance of generic systems for writers as members of a profession, a profession which changed over time but maintained a consensus of values which—however different specific opinions were at different times and in different places—offered a ready code of communication both among professionals and to their audiences. That generic concepts may be indispensable to literature in general E. D. Hirsch's interesting book more than suggests; E. H. Gombrich's theory of perception based on received and receivable schemata has implications far wider than the field of visual arts. Although I think and hope that these theorists are right, my own attempt remains narrower— simply to try to define some of the ways in which the idea of genre governed (—a vile phrase) and contributed to (—an O.K. phrase) writers and writing in one of the great outbursts of literary growth and change.

Although it seems obvious that a genre-system offers a set of interpretations, of "frames" or "fixes" on the world, and that some Renaissance genre-critics tried to fix those fixes hard, it was not entirely obvious in the Renaissance what the genres of literature surely were, nor yet how to identify them. From Aristotle onward, we keep hearing what "poetry," or imaginative literature, *isn't*: for Aristotle it wasn't oratory, or history, or philosophy; for most Renaissance critics, it wasn't medieval poetry and therefore wasn't Dante; for Ronsard and the Pléiade in sixteenth-century France, it wasn't Rabelais' *Gargantua et Pantagruel*; for Sidney, often generous in his categories, it wasn't plays which "be neither right Tragedies nor right Comedies; mingling Kings and Clownes"—a dictum which, taken seriously, would remove *Henry IV* and *King Lear* from critical attention. Nor was meter always enough to insure that a work was "poetry," even though many ancient genres were designated simply by their metrical arrangements —elegiacs, iambics, sapphics, alcaics, etc. Aristotle removed Empedocles from the canon, metrics and all, because philosophy did not involve *mimesis*, imaginative imitation, of reality, but describes truth, whereas history simply describes "fact." A modern Aristotelian, Julius Caesar Scaliger, let Empedocles back into the canon, together with other philosophical poets, and generalized the doctrine of mimesis to include in the epic category Heliodorus' prose *Ethiopian History*. Aristotle's stress on the categories of *poetry*, as distinct from other verbal conventions or systems, was Horace's stress also: from a mingling of these great texts grew the major tenets of Renaissance literary criticism. But neither these systems nor their components were identical—which meant that confusion underlay all Renaissance genre-theory, even the simplest.

Certainly critics could find evidence for the idea of genre in ancient texts wherever they looked, evidence which could be systematized and generalized in various ways. There were the *genera dicendi*, divisions into high and middle and low styles; there were metrical genres, which gave rise to many Renaissance theoretical experiments in vernacular quantitative verse; there were genres based on the rendering of a poem

—sung or spoken, accompanied or unaccompanied by what instrument; genres based on speaker or "voice"—the poet's own or his characters'. Vergil's dominance in medieval and later theory accounted for one application of the *genera dicendi* to his kinds in ascending order—low style-pastoral, middle-georgic, high-epic—which may in part explain to us why there is so very much pastoral poetry in the period, the kind with which poets officially "began," and beyond which many never passed. By Aristotle's law, though, georgics were not poetry at all, since they were descriptive rather than mimetic: the middle style must be reassigned. Tragedy-high style, comedy-middle; satire-low was one way of doing it—but then, where do the lyric genres go? Some, dithyramb or ode, seem higher in style than the pastoral lyric—or, to put it another way, odes seem more like heroic poetry and therefore candidates for a higher style than lyrics of love or banqueting.

In spite of the fact that Aristotle gave so good a model for literary definition that his editor Robortello could, simply by extrapolation, produce an Aristotelian definition for comedy matching the original definition for tragedy; in spite of the fact that Guarini could defend his uncanonical pastoral tragicomedy on impeccably Aristotelian lines against his Aristotelian enemies; in spite of the fact that the *Poetics* stated firmly what was poetry and what wasn't, offering reasons in each case; in spite of the fact that in that document an hierarchy of literary forms was set up, Aristotle was nonetheless far from an absolute or even a consistent guide to ancient genre-practice. Two kinds of institutions favor category and order, even in literature: schools, in one of which Aristotle was a distinguished teacher, and libraries. From the great library at Alexandria we can find traces of generic system—a familiar Dewey-decimal model, really, designed to store books and therefore to store knowledge. A poet, Callimachus, was charged with preparing the catalogue of the library (in the lost *Pinakes*). From the fragmentary references to this huge work and from Callimachus' own poetry, arranged categorically in Heroics, Hymns, Iambics, Epigrams, etc., we can read something of how that system worked: literary works were organized by groups, sometimes thematic (as in the category *Comic Poets,* of which the poet Lycophron was later keeper), sometimes metrical, sometimes topical; within a given group, works were organized by author when known, then generically; within genres they were alphabetically aligned. Apparently this sort of organization (most obviously reflected in the manuscripts of the Greek Anthology of epigrams recovered in the Renaissance) was understood and taken for granted by Horace and other Roman writers, engaged in imitating not only reality but (even more important) the literary forms in which their Greek models had imitated reality—hence Horace's relative clarity about generic forms in his *Ars poetica.*

We can understand these practical ways of keeping writing straight, since our own libraries are based on much the same principles, and there is considerable evidence elsewhere of both generic categorization and generic ranking. In the *Ion,* it is taken for granted that poetry comes in kinds, and in the *Republic* also. We find generic histories—Aristotle's of tragedy, Cicero's and Tacitus' short histories of oratory. Velleius Paterculus discussed the growth and decline of all the arts, in particular literature, and drew the parallel between the flowerings of fifth-century Athens and his native Rome. Cicero divided poetry into tragic, comic, epic, melic, and dithyrambic in the *De optimo genere oratorum,* where his famous regulation against mixing styles occurs: "in the kinds, each to his own tone and voice, which the educated recognize." Organization of this sort naturally encouraged the idea of competition, of overgoing—Cicero awarded prizes to particular poets for epic, tragic, and comic poetry; so did Horace, though to different winners. The potato race, the sack race, the three-legged race, are competitions of like ritual kind, but in the low style. Horace tells of his own development in a genre—first he wrote in Greek, then in his own Latin in imitation of Lucilius, beside whose satires, he says, his own are mere trifles. Still, his "trifles" draw fire: he tells us that some critics found his satires "nerveless," others that they exceeded the bounds set by the norm ("ultra legem tendere opus"). "Set by the norm"—there were, then, understood norms, with bounds, as we might also gather from Cicero's phrase about decorum in style, a decorum "known to the educated." The fact that the *concept* of generic form was taken for granted is more important than any definition of a specific generic norm could ever be, I think: Propertius seems to be speaking in thoroughly known categories when he tells us that he left the "buskin" of Aeschylus for his own "poems turned on a smaller lathe"—that is his love-elegies. We can find in Pliny comments on the genre of comedy, and Statius wrote about funeral themes and their forms. Ovid showed how his naughty subject, love, had invaded other genres (epic, tragic, comedy, etc.) and compared his verse, particularly the *Ars amatoria*, favorably with the *capricci* written on gambling, ball-games, swimming, cosmetics, and feasts—themes taken up in the Latin verse of the Renaissance and often very amusingly developed.

As is the case with anything taken for granted, tantalizingly little is explained of the literary system. We can tell, though, that imitation of Greek models was de rigueur for Roman poets, and that there were *kinds* of poetry to imitate. From Propertius' remark and from Callimachus' categories, we suspect, too that the *size* of a poem was important in generic definition. Moreover, the thematic stress of generic comment hinted sufficiently to Renaissance writers that cultural transfer was achieved by generic means; that Roman authors had so proceeded to domesticate Greek values, and that they might accomplish the same task in the same way.

To read the moving letters of Petrarca, obsessed with domesticating ancient literature in his own period and milieu, is to recognize how powerful was his conviction that *kind* offered the way to re-educate his generation. The correspondence between Boccaccio and Petrarca on literary themes conveys an eerie sense of their conviction of control over "everything"—they knew which texts were important, they trusted their diligent art to accommodate those crucial elements of ancient culture to their own world. Merely glancing down a list of their works, we can see how they accomplished this transfer in generic terms. Petrarca was romantic, or mythic, about it, writing his *Africa* in Latin, his provençal love-lyrics in the vernacular—writing his *Africa* indeed, mostly in Italy, his *Canzoniere* partly in Provence. His Scipio, symbol for the epic world, for Roman grandeur, and for the fusion of earthly and heavenly experience, was more than an epic hero for him, rather a hero transferring across time and space antique *numen* to Petrarca and by Petrarca's means to his own age. Geography counted: Boccaccio drew the Sicilian Muse from Sicily to that other Sicily, Naples, and thence to Florence in his *Ninfale Fiesolano*; Petrarca worked to endow his Helicon, the Sorgue, and his Tempe, the Vaucluse, with the numen of poetic significance. King Hugo of Cyprus, King Robert of Sicily, were invoked by these poets as imperial patrons had been, as imperial patrons to be: Petrarca arranged for his laureateship on the Capitoline, the archaeologically proper place for such crowning: he made himself into his myth.

But they were businesslike too: following what they believed to be Vergil's prescriptive model in the Eclogues, Petrarca and Boccaccio provided the Eclogues of their Carmina buc(c)olica with hidden meanings, which they scrupulously

revealed to their correspondents. In prose forms and poetic—
in discourse, dialogue, biography, geography, epistle, as well as
comedy, pastoral narrative, eclogues, triumphs, verse epistles,
etc.—these two men labored to present new models for good
literature to Europe as a whole and Florentines in particular,
always in generic form. Petrarca was fussy about genre: not
just any old "kind" pleased him; it had to be classical. Late
in life, he wrote to thank Boccaccio for the gift of the *Decameron*, but dismissed it as an early work of Boccaccio's
youth, before he had seen the light: The *Decameron* was written for an audience of ladies, on trivial topics—so much for
Boccaccio's generic distinction in the preface to the *Decameron*, "cento novelle, ò favole, ò parabole, ò historie." It was
Boccaccio's later work, the missionary work for antiquity,
that Petrarca honored, urging his friend to even greater efforts on behalf of humanism.

Petrarca insisted that the forms be restored in their purity,
and inveighed against the habit of florilegia, of anthologizing
piecemeal, which robbed readers, he felt, of any sense of a
work of literature as a made thing, as, literally, a poem. We
may note, too, that these two, at the beginning, were blissfully
unaware that certain ancient forms might not be fully poetic—
the dialogue, the discourse, the epistle: good humanists *avant
la lettre*, they took the forms they found and imitated them.
So the work, *mutatis mutandis*, was done everywhere: Du
Bellay runs through the acceptable kinds in his *Deffense*, Ronsard in his *Abrégé de l'art poétique française* and in the intro-
ductions to his various volumes of verse. In the Pléiade poets'
work we can read the care with which they categorized their
poetry and produced proper poetic models for France. Sometimes they are exact and scholarly—so the effort in epigram
and ode; sometimes they exploit the metaphorical thematics
of a kind—*Gaietez, les Soupirs, les Regrets* are the titles of
sonnet-collections; Du Bellay honored Petrarca in calling his

14

love-sonnets *Olive*. Ronsard's *Franciade,* Camoens' *Os Lusiadas* follow the Vergilian pattern in recording cultural transfer from one civilization to its successor; even as Vergil made Aeneas come from Troy to Latium, so Francion and Lusus came from Troy to France and Portugal. Lusus' descendant, Vasco da Gama, sailed out epically to transfer Portuguese culture in his turn. Geography mattered culturally, as it did for Petrarca, who mooned about Mantua thinking programmatically of Vergil. Ronsard's origins in the Vendôme, Du Bellay's in Anjou were constantly stressed in their poetry and by their readers; whose woods these are we know when Ronsard laments the felling in the Gâtine. It is Naples and its countryside which Sannazaro pastoralizes in his *Arcadia*— and from the notion of Naples, too, perhaps, he made his shepherds into fishermen. In Vergil's honor a writer of eclogues whose name was Spagnuoli called himself Mantuanus. Spenser mythicizes the Thames in the *Prothalamion,* the Irish landscape in the *Epithalamion;* Michael Drayton makes a geographical myth of his whole island in the historical-geographical-epical *Polyolbion.* Johannes Secundus' title, "Basia," makes generic metaphor of Catullus' wonderful word. Ronsard's *Bocages,* Jonson's *Timber* and *Underwoods* adapt the already metaphorical *Sylvae,* or mixed matter and mixed forms, of Statius, Poliziano, and others.

The idea of genre governed in another area too: the work of the great *librarii,* the booksellers, was no less organized by kind than the Alexandrian library had been. From the editions of Aldus Manutius and his sons, Henri Estienne and his sons, we see how automatically they organized by kind. Estienne's generic publications are particularly helpful for students of literature, then and now: in his huge collection of the Greek heroic poets, he included Bion, Moschus, and Theocritus, although he soon removed them along with a covering essay on Vergil's eclogues which brought the genre from Greece to

Rome, to a book called *Bucolica*. In one extra-Aristotelian commentary, *Poesis Philosophica*, Estienne collected fragments of Empedocles, Parmenides, Pythagoras, Musaeus, and others, together with the letters of Heraclitus and Democritus: genre is governed by subject here, in a volume important for several subsequent Renaissance efforts to write philosophy in verse. As he had with his eclogue collection, Estienne extended the category of philosophical poetry to include Lucretius. After publishing Aulus Gellius' *Attic Nights*, Estienne published his notes to that text as *Parisian Nights*, joking about the scholarly vigils he devoted to Aulus Gellius. The point is, these notes sketch an essay on kind: Estienne stressed the likeness in form—or better, in non-form—between the compendia of Aulus Gellius and Macrobius, and lamented that he had not managed to publish them together in one book (which would have been immense, of course). That is, his concern to put like works together extended beyond officially poetic forms to grant a principle of kind to all and any writing, an attitude characteristic of humanists who refused to allow some literary works to be considered more literary than others. Further, we can recognize in Estienne's notion a scholarly desire not yet entirely extinct: he wanted to put into a students' hands, within two covers, "all" the material on any given subject.

I caught on to this first—much later than I should have— when looking up material on horticulture as part of an effort to understand the background of allusion in Marvell's little poem, "The Garden"; and found Cato, Varro, Columella, the ancient authorities on agriculture, reliably printed together for my convenience in volumes usually called *De re rustica*. Gradually I found Vergil's *Georgics* joining the first triad, occasionally also Poliziano's poem on gardens and Palladio's text on the proper organization of country estates. Looking up books on military theory, in order to write one clause in the third lecture of this series, I found ancient authorities together in volumes called *De re militaria,* and not only learnt about Sir Thomas Browne, my *point de départ,* but also understood a good deal more about Fluellen, that country gentleman whose hobby was the discipline of ancient warfare, in which boys were not needlessly killed. In my long preoccupation with the subliterary form of rhetorical paradox, I became accustomed to finding the same authorities invoked in the apologetic prefaces to new paradoxes, but found as well various combinations of these same authorities dished up categorically in volumes designed for delectation and imitation. It made my work easier—as it did Robert Burton's, who owned a book in which Erasmus' *Praise of Folly,* together with his defense of it to Martinus Dorp, was bound up with Seneca's, Calcagnini's, and Synesius' paradoxes against received opinion, all ready to hand for the *Anatomy of Melancholy.*

We may take it, then, that literary invention—both "finding" and "making"—in the Renaissance was largely generic, and that transfer of ancient values was largely in generic terms, accomplished by generic instruments and helps. So the work was done elsewhere—in Lyons with the early printers, in Paris with the Pléiade, even in England by the Sidney circle and more independent souls. Very late in the Renaissance, at the beginning of the seventeenth century, Pieter Cornelisz. Hooft determined to bring the vernacular literature of his young country, the hardly-United Netherlands, into the modern world. To do so he set to work, civic humanist that he was, by translating great works, notably Tacitus' history, which he then made the formal and moral model for his own *History of the Netherlands.* He produced formal tragedies and a Plautine comedy, a romantic Ariostan tragedy, and an interlude on the Judgment of Paris: the range, then, of dramatic forms. If we add to this his *Joyeuse Entrée* for the young Mary Stuart, come to marry William II, we reach into the area of triumphal pageant-drama of medieval celebration, brought up-to-date by the decorations of classical triumphs. Hooft wrote in most of the modern lyric forms, too: songs, sonnets, emblems, verse epistles à la Ovid, eclogues, epigrams, epithalamia, anniversaries, elegies, genethliaca, odes, entertainments for public persons, celebrations of public events. What Hooft left undone (with one significant exception) his younger contemporary Constantijn Huygens scrupulously did. Huygens wrote a fine topographical poem in praise of his native town, The Hague; a long satire; and a pastoral lament which managed to incorporate public policy and a complex self-analytical dialogue between the now-silent shepherd and the poet himself. In addition, Huygens translated parts of Guarini's *Pastor Fido*; he wrote a highly successful farce in Antwerp dialect; and he provided the first character-poems in Europe. He worked in large forms, which he made very discursive; he contributed a great deal of autobiography to his poetry, writing a long poem on his tiny countryhouse, Hofwyck—a long paeon to his public enterprise in constructing a paved road between the fishing village Scheveningen and the Hague. His family poem managed to make compatible domestic economy (with prayers for family and servants) and cosmology; late in his life, he constructed a Latin verse-autobiography. With all this, he wrote epithalamia, genethliaca, elegies, epitaphs, epicedia, and epigrams by the hundred. He translated some of Donne's, Marino's, and Théophile's poems into Dutch; he wrote devotional poems of varying lengths, as well as important devotional sonnets; at the very end of his life, he wrote a physicotheological poem on the comet of 1680–1681, in which he readjusted the Ptolemaic cosmology he had presented as true fifty years before, to make plain that he now dwelt in a new universe with his gifted son, the astronomer and physicist Christiaen Huygens.

We may note the absence of epic in the Dutch list: there

is no unfinished *Franciade* or *Faerie Queene* here: there is, too, a reason for that lack, I think. Like Boccaccio and Petrarca, Hooft and Huygens turned their native literature around, forced it to take its place on the European continent as a respectable, sophisticated vernacular. But they did this three hundred years after Petrarca began his ambitious project in the same line; in one generation, Hooft and Huygens traversed the accomplishment of those three hundred years, so that not only were the forms and kinds introduced to Holland, but so also were the styles, developing over time, of those forms and kinds. By many scholars, Huygens is classed as a "baroque" poet (whatever that may be)—not as "Renaissance" at all. In his work much is telescoped: where Petrarca had insisted on the purity of each genre, unmixed with another, and Hooft had largely kept to that program, Huygens offers us *genera mista* in almost every case—self-conscious, carefully worked mixtures, which counterpoint against one another the separate genres Petrarca was trying to reestablish. "If severed they be good, the conjunction cannot be hurtfull," Huygens learnt from Sidney.

I turn now to mixed genre as a mode of *thought* as well as of poetry, and to that same Cicero who was so firm in separating generic styles from one another. In Cicero's *De Oratore*, the orator Crassus laments the decay of the arts from that golden time in which Hippias of Elis could boast "that there was nothing in any art at all that he did not know, that not only did he know all the arts of a liberal education—geometry, music, letters, and poetry, as well as the teachings of natural science, ethics, and politics, but indeed he had made with his own hands the ring he had on, the cloak he was clad in, the boots he wore."

"There are," Crassus went on, "other losses to the arts, by being split up into several parts. Do you imagine that in the time of Hippocrates of Cos, there were some doctors who specialized in medicine, others in surgery, still others in diseases of the eye? Or that geometry for Euclid or Archimedes, or music for Damon or Aristoxenus, or letters for Aristophanes or Callimachus were so separate that no one could comprehend the *genus universum*—culture as a whole, the total kind—but rather that everyone chose a different slice of a subject for his specialty?" It is this *genus universum*, culture as a whole, to which Sidney refers in his great topical paean to poetry as fundamental to all culture, any civilization; and, indeed, this is why the library at Alexandria was called Museion, because it housed *all* the muses, not just the literary ones. In a book published in 1541, Mario Equicola organized learning in nine categories, each governed by one of the muses; the cosmos, the topics of study and of poetry, the *coelicoli* were all related to one muse or another, and for each category there was also an assigned literary kind.

In his *Defence*, again and again Sidney reiterates, always in generic lists, his belief that the *paideia* is born *as* poetry and borne *by* poetry—Musaeus created dithyramb and prophecy, Homer heroic matter, Hesiod theogony and agriculture, Orpheus and Linus hymns and prophetic poetry, Amphion architecture, Thales, Empedocles and Parmenides philosophy, Pythagoras and Phocylides ethics, Solon politics, Plato philosophy and dramatic dialogue, Herodotus history ("entituled by the name of the nine Muses"): these are the heroes of civilization and of poetry, gigantic *inventores* and recorders of the kinds of knowledge and of art. Their efforts taken together makes up the *genus universum*; along with Antonio Minturno, Scaliger, William Webbe and a host of others, Sidney presents the whole *paideia* as poetic topics.

And so thought many humanist literary theorists opposed to the limiting tendency of Renaissance Aristotelian-Horatians, who carefully defined the genres and wrote out of the poetic canon much of the matter given above in Sidney's list. Minturno insisted that philosophy and poetry *were* in fact poetic: Empedocles, Lucretius, Lucan were poets, and so were writers on various arts—Hesiod and Vergil on agriculture; Horace, Vida, Fracastoro on poetry. After listing the different literary kinds, Minturno proceeded to show how they were and could be mixed: epic, for instance, has parts that are elegiac, epigrammatic, hymnic; Petrarca's *Trionfi* are clearly heroic, if not epic; and bucolics, he thought, fronted on epic (he cited Boccaccio's *Ameto* and Sannazaro's *Arcadia*). His own *Amor innamorato*, a mixture of prose with poetry, treats of heroic love. A host of inclusionist critics could be grouped with Minturno and Sidney—Francesco Patrizi (like E. D. Hirsch) argued that every poem on any subject had its poetic kind; and that "misti poemi" were valuable precisely because they combined various "sets" on the world into a larger collective vision. Joannes Antonius Viperano suggested that it was always possible to make a new genre, as one could see from the many extant works which mixed the kinds. He noted (*pace* Thomas Rosenmeyer) that bucolics had become very mixed in subject matter and in form, and that the epic had always been so; Giovanni Pietro Capriano, Equicola, Benedetto Varchi, Speroni, Guarini and his allies variously defended a large number of genres—which they considered necessary instruments of interpreting reality, to render all there is, in heaven and on earth. Varchi also argued for adapting to literary kinds the categories of the other arts, music and painting in particular.

Though he contributed to the literature of *paragone*, of competition among the arts (see Aristotle's protracted argument about epic and tragic poetry), as well as the many Renaissance *paragoni* among the visual arts (a theme borrowed from antiquity), Varchi's chief interest lay not in the rivalries among art-forms and disciplines but in their contributions to one another. In one musician's borrowing from the literary genre-system as he understood it, I hope to show how solid and reliable this very indefinable system could be. Claudio Monteverdi, inheritor of a highly developed union of music and poetry in the dominant madrigal-form, recognized the stylistic changes in the lyric between Petrarca's time and Marino's sufficiently to exploit their possibilities for his madrigal art: most of his innovative work was done on texts by writers *he* considered to have been innovators in poetry, as he was an innovator in music. He chose Tasso, Guarini, and Marino as poets whose texts could lead him into more complex musical creations. When he turned later to texts by Petrarca and Bembo, set *ad infinitum* in the generation of madrigalists just preceding his own, Monteverdi deliberately tried to recognize their archaism in a stylistic "progression" within the madrigal genre, and to overgo the achievements of earlier madrigalists who had set these same texts. He went farther, using Ovidian literary forms and rhetorical techniques to translate his *lamenti* into music—Arianna's for Baccho, Orfeo's for Euridice, the Virgin's for her dead Son. In his new form, *Tirsi e Clori*, Monteverdi consciously set himself to the pathos of pastoral rendering, moving into a new genre of music; he repeated the operation, higher on the stylistic scale, in his musical version of what amounts to a short epic, the episode from *Gerusalemme Liberata* of Tancredi's duel with Clorinda. By his accomplishment, we can recognize in the literary genre-system a sufficiently secure scheme for the invention— the finding—of a musical equivalent. From his understanding of the separate musical and literary kinds, too, we can the better understand how Monteverdi mixed the literary and musical kinds in what is *the* mixed genre in the arts, the opera.

From the clear and frank mixture of genres in the opera, we may appropriately look back upon the fountainhead of western literature, to Homer once more. In a Plutarchian tradition, Renaissance theorists found "all" in Homer—not only had he written an epic (the *Iliad*) which gave rise to the tragic genre, but also he had written an epic from which comedy sprang, in the *Odyssey*; from comedy to romance was but a short step. Even Aristotle recognized several "kinds" in Homer's work, and derived comedy from the mock-epic *Margites* attributed to Homer in antiquity. Throughout the Renaissance, the kinds were fathered or grandfathered on Homer—satire (Scaliger), hymns (Minturno), orations (everyone), epigrams, as well as the history and philosophy banned by Aristotle from the canon. It is easy to sympathize with the anti-Aristotelian Patrizi's remark that, by Aristotelian standards, only one half of the *Iliad* might be considered poetry. In other words, Homer *was* the *paideia*, the model for education; and the way to education, even with only Homer as a textbook, was by kind. Taken thematically, or as disciplines within the *paideia*, the poetic kinds had existed as long as civilization had: indeed, poets were the *inventores* of civilization. Sidney listed the vatic bards whose poems both formed and contained civilization: that the list was rattled off by Minturno, Equicola, Scaliger, William Webbe and many others only demonstrates the strength of that topical notion, and makes even plainer why Milton wanted to write a poem "doctrinal to the nation." If one wishes to be economical about the kinds, then they may all be seen as latent within the work of another mythic founder of a tradition, Homer. No wonder the epic seemed so mixed a form in the Renaissance— and, also, no wonder there were such battles over Dante, Ariosto, and Tasso! No wonder, too, that mock-epics began to make fun of such totality, and a comic prose-epic to criticize the criticism as well.

Within the idea of a genre-system, then, various notions of genre competed for attention and imitation—Sidney's *Defence* lists the kinds by substance as well as by form. In the *artes poeticae* of the late sixteenth and early seventeenth centuries, we often find a list of possible forms, with their distinctions drawn in terms of topic or content. Ronsard's friendly address to his readers will do as a sample:

> Tu dois sçavoir que toute sorte de Poësie a l'argument propre à son subject: l'Heroïque, armes, assaults de villes, batailles, escarmouches, conseils et discours des capitaines; la Satyrique, brocards et repréhensions de vices; la Tragique, morts et misérables accidents de Princes; la Comique, la license effrenée de la jeunesse, les ruses des courtizannes, avarice de vieillards, tromperie de valets; la Lyrique, l'amour, le vin, les banquets dissolus, les danses, masques, chevaux victorieux, escrime, joustes et tournois, et peu souvent quelque argument de Philosophie. Pource, Lecteur, si tu vois telles matières librement escrites, et plusieurs fois redites en ces Odes, tu ne t'en dois esmerveiller, mais toujours te souvenir des vers d'Horace en son Art poëtique:

> *Musa dedit fidibus Divos, puerosque Deorum,*
> *Et pugilem victorem et equum certamine primum,*
> *Et juvenum curas, et libera vina referre.*

By this kind of definition, form implies context and, indeed, context implies a particular form. "I sing" implies "the wrath of Achilles," "of Arms and the Man who," or "Of Mans first Disobedience, and. . . ," just as the reed pipe, the syrinx, *la sampogna*, implies the pastoral "set." The important thing about these generic phrases, taken as it were from the grammar of epic in this case, is that they imply each other; we can reverse the business too: "Arma virumque" implies "cano," and we must await Milton's "I sing" at the end of the long, complicated clause with which *Paradise Lost* begins. Such reliance takes a genre-system for granted, as *donnée*: from genre so interpreted Monteverdi borrowed. Within its securities, Robert Herrick, supremely a poet of the little in subject and form, can write his variations:

> I sing of Brooks, of Blossomes, Birds, and Bowers:
> Of April, May, of June and July-flowers.
> I sing of May-poles, Hock-carts, Wassails, Wakes,
> Of Bride-grooms, Brides, and of their Bridall-cakes.
> I write of Youth, of Love, and have Accesse
> By these, to sing of cleanly-Wantonnesse.
> I sing of Dewes, of Raines, and piece by piece,
> Of Balme, of Oyle, of Spice, and Amber-Greece.
> I sing of Times trans-shifting; and I write
> How Roses first came Red, and Lillies White.
> I write of Groves, of Twilights, and I sing
> The Court of Mab, and of the Fairie-King.
> I write of Hell; I sing (and ever shall)
> Of Heaven, and hope to have it after all.

Nothing could less satisfactorily fulfill the epic "I sing"; the brooks, blossoms, birds, bowers are the pastoral so radiant in Herrick's book, *Hesperides*. The May-poles and Hock-carts refer to celebrations in the rhythm of a georgic year; brides and bridegrooms appear in pro- and epithalamia; dews and rains in philosophical or scientific poetry; times trans-shifting in allegorical, historical, or metamorphic poetry; and "How Roses first came Red, and Lillies White" points not only to specific poems in the *Hesperides* but also to Herrick's distinguished exercise in diminution, reducing Ovidian metamorphic topics to epigram size. Groves are the numinous *loci* of supernatural presence; "the Court of Mab, and of the Fairie-King" (Oberon) diminishes Spenser's epic story to thumbnail scale. With "I write of Hell; I sing (and ever shall) Of Heaven," we return to the epic promise of the first words, now translated into sacred story—and realize that Herrick *has* in fact given all that he promised in the secular *Hesperides* (that mixed garden) and in the sacred *Noble Numbers*. By choosing the epigram as his major poetic form, Herrick has reduced the pretensions of genres "large" in scope or theme or size—has mocked them, treated them as metaphors, even as he exploits their official topics. So with his invocation "To His Muse": this "Mad maiden" isn't invited to descend to the poet, rather she is urged to sit still, to stop running away from the poet (now decently countrified) to the wicked and seductive city whence he has come. He encourages her to sit still "In poore and private Cottages," where her "meaner Minstrelsie," called an intermixture of "Eclogues and Beucolicks," will be appreciated for what it is and not subjected to the destructive comments of urban critics. That is, Herrick's pastoral muse is conceived as yearning for her generic and dialectic opposite, the city, even as the poet, discontented occasionally in Devon, has settled for Devon and its natural beauty.

Without a genre-system to play against, all this falls flat. Herrick relies upon a literary system readers can take for granted, works with professional commonplaces in a professionally common place, occupied by readers as well as writers who understand what is expected of them. Without awareness of the decorum supplied by a system of genres something like what Ronsard and North rattled off, such poetry as this makes almost no sense, and Herrick seems the poet of trivia so many have taken him for. With an awareness of the games played with his own poetic traditions, he can seem a considerable craftsman at the very least, and a considerable innovator at the very best. There are many other examples of similar reliance on the system which in fact subvert the system. Giambattista Marino showed his skill in various ways— in the short epic, *La Strage de gli Innocenti*; in a long Ovidian poem, *L'Adone*; in lyric forms named for their proper instrument, *La Lira* and *La Sampogna*. But he wrote another book, unlike most books I know, called *La Galeria*. The subdivisions of this book are named for the topics of the poems—*Pittura, Scultura*. Within these broad terms there are more precise ones—ritratti, portraits of popes, princes, cardinals, captains, heroes, tyrants, pirates, magicians and heretics, Greek, Latin, and modern poets, beautiful women good and bad, as well as burlesque portraits (interestingly enough, of burlesque or mocking poets, Folengo and Pulci); historical paintings (really mythological, in our terminology); narrative paintings, chiefly of biblical subjects; and finally *capricci* (on an ant, a glowworm, a mosquito). The statues were also divided into categories—reliefs, medals, and again capricci, or grotesque topics. By this ecphrastic book, Marino raises the whole question of generic division; he divides and subdivides, affecting to suit style to subject—but in fact all these elaborately categorized poems are simply epigrams, written from the low style to the highest. Not only that, all these subjects are *normal* epideictic topics: we do not need the pictures and statues (some of them imaginary, others actual works of art) for such poems. Marino is playing a joke, pretending to categorical arrangement for which he had no real need. By asserting unnecessary categorical determinations, Marino makes us think back to recognize afresh that the arts have different semiotic systems, and that they are, as individual disciplines, important for that very difference. He is making fun of the doctrine *ut pictura poesis*, and catches us unaware by breaking down an apparent difference from art to art while keeping firmly to his own medium.

Taking the critic and theorist Julius Caesar Scaliger as a test-case for a moment, I want to discuss some of the ways in which a genre-system can maintain and also subvert its own rules. Scaliger's *Poetices libri septem* is generically organized. Sometimes he writes within one genre-system—metrics, for instance—but his chief interest in the genres was topical or thematic. Hence, though in one sense he is a good Renaissance Aristotelian critic, in other ways he was an unregenerate independent: for example, he allowed imaginative prose to be literature and refused to deny philosophy a place in poetics. Close definer that he was of the decorums of different genres, he also argued for works mixed in kind. Scaliger may have been one authority for Sidney's argument for *genera mista*:

> Now in his parts, kindes, or Species (as you list to terme them), It is to be noted that some Poesies have coupled together two or three kindes, as Tragicall and Comicall, whereupon is risen the Tragicomicall. Some in the like manner have mingled Prose and Verse, as Sanazzar and Boetius. Some have mingled matters Heroicall and Pastoral [Sidney himself, in his *Arcadia*]. But that commeth all to one in this question, for if severed they be good, the conjunction cannot be hurtfull.

Without losing sight of the specific requirements for generic division, Scaliger at the same time defends the propositions that everything utterable has its genre, and that a complex, large, inclusive utterance may require mixture of the kinds. That is, I think Scaliger recognizes the principle of invariancy, which assures a given genre its subject and style, and in some cases shape also, as well as the inclusiveness dictated by belief in the *paideia*; within his genre-system, he allows for countergenericism too. Not in the least discounting the importance of formal arrangements, Scaliger nonetheless stresses subject matter as the definer of kind, a stress which leads inevitably to the generic thematics recognized by Monteverdi's adaptation to another art of the literary genre-system. It leads as well out of genre to *mode*, where thematics and style often predominate over form and forms.

Another way of saying all this is that Scaliger followed through the implications of his *comparative* criticism. He took for granted the periodization of literature, as well as the historical transfers of culture effected by literary means; he recognized the rivalry as well as the imitation of Greek writings by Romans, of ancient writings by moderns. Not for nothing did he make his endless "comparationes" of Vergil with his Greek counterparts, Ennius with his, Ovid and Horace with theirs; not for nothing, in a section called "Hypercritica," did he compare modern writers with the ancients. Recognizing generic distinctions—that is to say, interpreting and criticizing texts categorically—Scaliger allows himself to be a critic, to make judgments on the texts he discussed. By multiplying his systematic examinations, he could consider all the available writings of the three civilizations *as a whole*, a universal kind, called "literature." That is, he can handle literature synchronically or diachronically—and could have done neither without a very strong sense of history, of alteration and modification over time.

By ending this section on the generic inclusionism which we do not always expect genre-theory to permit, but which turns up constantly in Renaissance genre-commentary, I allow my own interests and sympathies to show. I would like to present genre-theory as a means of accounting for connections between topic and treatment within the literary system, but also to see the connection of the literary kinds with *kinds* of knowledge and experience; to present the kinds as a major part of that *genus universum* which is part of all literary students' heritage. The kinds honor aspects and elements of culture and in their conjunctions help make up culture as a whole. In the liminal poem to Herrick's *Hesperides* cited earlier, "I sing of Brooks, etc.," we can see the Homeric *hubris* at work, as into those tiny forms which make up his book Herrick wrote in as many different kinds as Homer in his mighty epic. Conscious of his place in a poetic heritage and a poetic profession, Herrick demonstrated his poet's aims: aesthetically, to vary his work; professionally, to master his craft and to surprise us with that mastery; humanly, to render the variety, the *sylva* or mixed matter of experience. And all this not in a book called *Sylvae* or *Forrest* or *Underwoods*, but in a book whose title holds another kind of richness, more delicate, more cultivated, more various—*Hesperides*, the garden of the Gods, of love, of generation, of reward.

Herrick's view of genre seems to me a good paradigm for my own: patterns, kinds, mental sets organize for us the lives we individually lead, much as these kinds, sets, patterns organized the vast body of literature. Experience can be seen as searching for its own form, after all: the kinds may act as myth or metaphor for a man's new vision of literary truth. To go from one type of epigram to another, let me cite the German humorist Roda-Roda, whose *Kleine Literaturege-schichte* (really *Literaturtheorie*) sums up our problem beautifully "Ein Mann allein: ein lyrisches Gedicht; zwei Maenner: eine Ballade; ein Mann und eine Frau: ein Novelle; ein Mann und zwei Frauen: ein Roman; eine Frau und zwei Maenner: eine Tragödie; zwei Frauen und zwei Maenner: ein Lustspiel." One might add, in an era of womens' lib, a category apparently inconceivable to Roda-Roda, *eine Frau allein*: in the high style, a volume of confessional poetry; in the middle style, a cookbook; in the low style, a narrative of successful call-girling. Which is to say: though there are generic conventions all right, they are also metastable. They change over time, in conjunction with their context of systems. At the time of writing, an author's generic concept is in one sense historical, in that he looks back at models to imitate and to outdo. The work he writes may alter generic possibilities (as *Don Quixote* did for western fiction) almost beyond recognition. So Diderot, so Stendhal, so Joyce—and so, I imagine, Homer too. But the writer's view is also synchronic in that he considers the array of relevant works as important for him *now*, not himself as the bearer of their traditions.

A different expression of Roda-Roda's view (together with its dialectical opposite) comes from *Don Quixote*, where literary vision is in constant competition (*paragone!*) with actual life. Some episodes in that book arrange themselves in their generic pattern and decorum, others crack along conventional fissures. The goatherds live as hard pastoralists must; Gines de Pasamonte is the picaroon he himself defines for the first time —but the windmills are windmills. "Take care, your worship," says Sancho; "those things over there are not giants but windmills, and what may seem to be their arms are sails, which are whirled around in the wind to make the millstones turn." "It is quite clear," said Don Quixote, "that you are not experienced in this matter of adventures. They are giants, and if you are afraid, go away and say your prayers, whilst I advance and engage them in fierce and unequal combat."

"Fierce and unequal combat": by the romance-topos taken as given Don Quixote understands the battering he is to get, justifies whatever happens. He knows his genre from the inside out; his genre is his fix on the world. In *Don Quixote*, indeed, reality is respected even as literary imagination is shown to be coterminous with life. When the old knight, defeated past endurance, has been (out of kindness) confined to his village for a year, he conceives a way of putting this idleness to use, by calling it *otium* and persuading his comrades to change their names and genre from the field to fields. His housekeeper and his niece overhearing him, put a stop to his enterprise as unbefitting the decorum of his age—and thereby kill Don Quixote, for whom, as for his master, literary kind was essential to any imaginative life.

II
Small Forms: Multo in Parvo

In Callimachan tradition, I want to discuss the functions of various forms of Renaissance writing which have in common only the fact of their relative smallness, and examine some of their implications for *genus universum,* culture as a whole, as well as suggest some interpenetration of one another by these forms. That is, I want to begin with the notion of the *paideia,* to start with culture, and to move into interpretation, if not criticism, at the end of this chapter. The tendency to mythicize genre noted earlier was counterbalanced by a strong tendency toward metaphorizing it: both covertly exploit the thematic associations of the different kinds. Scaliger was a major definer of generic themes, who overtly worked toward mixing and altering genres. Though Scaliger was good on definitions—an epicedium to be spoken over a body as yet unburied, epitaph over a buried body, an anniversary spoken a year or two years after the death, etc.—his emphasis on the subjects and themes of the genres he accepted carried him logically to consider shared generic frontiers and the overlap of generic specialties in *genera mista.* His ways of thinking about genre, in other words, led him toward modes and modal divisions of literature based on thematics.

Scaliger handled thematic and generic likenesses and convergences very well, but was less interested in mixtures of kind based on opposition. From a modern critic and scholar, Claudio Guillén, I borrow the notion of paired genres, or genre and countergenre, which he has laid out in exemplary fashion in his study of Cervantes' definition and use of the picaresque novel (as a form and as a mode) in the larger generic structure of *Don Quixote*. In another essay, Guillén has offered us a view of the picaresque itself emergent countergenerically to pastoral romance—the picaresque, then, as the dialectical development of a new form. I want to touch on all these disparate points in this essay, so I lay them all out now, to refer the more lightly to them at various moments later.

First of all, a sub-literary small form intended to transfer culture and to communicate important values, more a literary "device" than a genre, and workable into any kind of literature an author might choose. This is the adage, the *sententia*, a quotation from an authoritative source (biblical, classical, proverbial) which sums up a mass of experience in one charged phrase, demonstrating the community of human experience—in short, the adage is *literally* a common place, a convergence-point of consensus. The great textbook with this specialty was Erasmus' *Adagia—Adagiorum Chiliades*, or thousands of adages, which grew from a small collection of phrases from reputable classical texts into an immense compendium, multi-indexed, of hundreds of familiar phrases like *festina lente, Thersitae facies, Silenus Alcibiades*, and (my favorite) *delphinum cauda ligas* (catch a whale by the tail). Exactly as Petrarca deplored, Erasmus collected a patchwork, a mixed florilegium of ancient wisdom to make culture generally available; in his *De Copia* and *Colloquies*, Erasmus taught European schoolboys how to make use of his adages to best rhetorical advantage. The adages, then, become *ornament, copia*, figures for alluding to a large meaning from an important context. They are keys to culture, or convenient agents of cultural transfer.

The book, *Adagia*, stands as a compendium of ancient wisdom, seeming to deliver up into our hands a whole system of knowledge, offering readers the sense that an entire intellectual and social world has been condensed into its abbreviations. An adage bears a coded message, compresses much experience into a very small space; and by that very smallness makes its wisdom so communicable. Trust in adages and axioms can be noted in many different contexts, literary and intellectual, in our period—in Pico's condensed propositions drawn from the sum of available knowledge, 900 theses biblical, scholastic, Platonic, Aristotelian, Zoroastrian, Chaldean, etc., etc., which, for all their variety, Pico intended to relate to a single area of truth. In Bacon's substitution of new axioms for old in his *Novum Organum* we can see quite another manifestation of the truth of epigrammatic sentence: we recognize the tendency in a host of political and economic aphorisms designed to make sense of an altering economy, and in the proverbs of which Rabelais, Cervantes, Burton can make whole chapters in their books.

Since Erasmus was a scholar quite aware that his readers generally were not, he sidestepped the temptation to universal charlatanry and indicated his sources; that is, his compendium was not only a key to accumulated ancient wisdom, but it also unlocked ancient texts too—the book was a true medium of its own culture. In explaining "Thersitae facies," a trope for prodigious deformity, Erasmus tells us who Thersites was in the *Iliad*, and that he got his phrase not from Homer but from Suidas. "Evitata Charybdi in Scyllam incidi"—avoiding Charybdis only to fall into Scylla—allowed him to write a history of the commonplace, giving the story in the *Odyssey*, the geographical location (with sources cited) of those nautical hazards, and the points in Sallust, Horace, Vergil, Plato, and Plutarch where references to the situation occur, with explanations of their relevance. "Bis puer senex," an old man twice a child, is an adage Erasmus himself used powerfully in his *Praise of Folly*; *Falstaff* bandied the concept with Hal; and its tragic implications are laid out in *King Lear*. Erasmus tells us that the phrase comes from Varro, and that we can find other versions in Aristophanes, Sophocles, Plato, Lucian, Aristotle, Euripides, etc., etc., etc. No wonder we find Erasmus' adages everywhere—in Rabelais, of course, in Du Bellay's poetry, in Montaigne's essays, in Burton's *Anatomy*, as well as larding the speech of such intellectuals as Polonius and the Earl of Gloucester.

Erasmus' remarks on his adages were not merely scholarly; he also wrote about the phrase and sometimes even used it as he intended others to do, to spark off an essay of his own, as in the great essay on Christianity he composed on *Silenus Alcibiadis*. His tracts for the times are rare, though; in his apparatus Erasmus usually instructs us by restoring to his adages some of the context he had shorn away simply by choosing them.

Interestingly enough, Montaigne began his essays in much the same way, as remarks in the service of carefully selected adages. His own powerful personality, however, soon swamped such objective aims, and the adages he used throughout his essays occur more as the thematic punctuation Erasmus intended than as epigraphs to their own explication. Again and again, the adages return readers to a milestone marking Montaigne's errant and ambling way; these reliable remnants of antiquity allow readers to take their bearings upon the landscape of Montaigne's mind. Montaigne's use of such tags varied greatly: an essay (e.g., "Of Readie or Slow Speech," "Of Feare," "Of the Force of the Imagination") may begin with a tag, which for a while it explicates, before going its own independent way; or it may be nailed down in a crucial summary quotation. The essays "To Philosophize, is to learne how to die," and "Of Friendship" are studded with tags from clas-

sical prooftexts—but there is rather more of Horace and less of Seneca than one might expect in the first essay, and Cicero appears less often than I expected in the second—which means, I think, that Montaigne was aware of the purpose of adages and often shook readers' expectations in his deployment of them. Sometimes he deliberately finesses: in "A Consideration upon Cicero," there is no direct quotation from that author; in the well-known essay on the regulation of the libido, "Upon some Verses of Vergil," quotations occur from Ovid, Petronius, Martial, Seneca, Ennius, Cicero, Horace, Cornelius Gallus, Plato, and others before (eight pages into the essay) the verses from Vergil finally appear. We have come a long way from Erasmus' directness, even from his honest vagaries in those adage-comments where he tells us about himself: the point is, we might not have had these *Essais* at all without the *Adagia* and the adage-habit.

By beginning with adages, I have tried to suggest how a sub-genre of literature, the anthology of saws deriving from literary texts, and in some measure the vials of their thematic essence, was of ultimate service to Renaissance literature, feeding it in many ways. The essay is, really, in part a fulfillment of the implications of adage-making; by working from adages into new context, it developed into a form of its own.

Besides the essay, another kind new in the Renaissance owed part of its existence to the adage: this was the emblem. Though it is the pictorial part of the emblem which modern students chiefly notice, we know that the creator of the form, Andrea Alciato, began simply by combining two short forms, adage with epigram: it was his publisher who conceived the idea of adding figures, or woodcut pictures, to make the idea of the emblem easier to grasp for readers with small Latin and less Greek. Still, its pictorial aspect gave the emblem its peculiar force: though it is true that there are collections of adage-plus-epigram without visual apparatus which are called *emblemata,* the striking thing about the new collective form was its picture. It is important to note how this tiny form mixed genres and even arts—and how cryptic its parts were, implying far more than was said. With its gnomic grammatical involution of significance into one phrase, the adage offered one version of much in little; the epigram's syntactical economies challenged ingenuity precisely by its terseness. The addition of figures to such abbreviated forms might have opened up the emblem to a public potentially frustrated by its verbal tightness, as Alciato's publishers hoped; or, which in fact was what happened, the emblem might present a problem thrice made intricate and esoteric. Certainly early emblem-books exploit the enigmatic potentialities of the form; and theory was developed which stated that no part of the emblem—figure, epigram, caption or adage—was supposed to translate any other: rather all the elements were by their special means to point inward to a single idea, supported in part by them all. As the adage had done, then, the emblem stresses its own idea; far more than the adage, the emblem mimics the theory of the hieroglyph, a presentation of truth veiled, to be understood only by the initiate or the piercing reader.

Early emblems provide us with an almost perfect sample of esotericism. Verbal puns and images yoked by violence together served to express the particular intricacy of ideas demanding real effort on the part of the reader to unravel. Naturally enough, such a novelty as the emblem affected existing forms of poetry—among the good commentary bearing on the relations of emblems to poetry is Paul Alpers' helpful comment on Spenser's use of iconographical techniques. For Spenser and other poets—Crashaw, Lope de Vega, Marino— the emblem affected poetic practice in two ways: its condensation of meaning contributed to the intensity of some highly visual poetic vignettes, and its expectation of the reader's effort

toward revelation modified expression in poems not particularly visually emblematic. I want to look at the use of emblems
by two poets, who (I think anyway) got at the theory of the
emblem and translated it successfully, although very different-
ly one from the other, into their poetry.

The emblem-symbol works allusively, drawing in a whole
area of association not necessarily explored directly in a poem,
as Marvell uses such emblems in his microcosmic macrocosm,
his generic anthology, "Upon Appleton House." There, in a
long nature-episode, the speaker retires into a magic wood
where he is vouchsafed an experience of unity with nature. He
sees various natural creatures in a series of emblematic tab-
leaux, of which, he assures us, he understands the deepest secret
significances. But he doesn't quite tell us what those significances are, although we can invade this privacy a bit by looking
at actual analogues in emblem-books—the nightingale in-
structing her young in song (fig. 1); nuptial doves seeking
solitude in the woods, as the Fairfaxes, the noble pair whose
estate and whose daughter Marvell celebrates, sought solitude
in their country house (fig. 2); the heron mysteriously sacrificing her first nestling; the woodpecker bringing down a
tainted oak. All these symbolic natural actions make sense
to the poet, who understands "everything" about his arklike
wood:

> Give me but Wings as they, and I
> Streight floting on the Air shall fly;
> Or turn me but, and you shall see
> I was but an inverted Tree.

His Solomonic mystical experience in the "light Mosaick" of
Nunappleton's dappled wood permits him to comprehend
the speech of birds, to recognize each individual leaf in the
forest. But *we* cannot, for the poet does not let us in on the
hieroglyphic code. Not until we have done a lot of work in

Fig. 1. The nightingale teaching its young to sing.
Camerarius, *Symbolorum et emblematum . . . centuriae.*

Fig. 2. Nuptial doves retiring to the woods. Camerarius, *Symbolorum et emblematum . . . centuriae.*

old books (which, I must suppose, were in the Fairfax library) do we discover that Marvell has relied on emblematic meanings established with some fixedness—and also, that he has tacitly extended, conflated, and altered the conventional meanings attached to those particular creatures. The "elders" stoop to listen to the nightingale in this poem as parent-nightingales apparently do in life; but these elders are also the normally thornless bushes which in the poem's miraculous ecology retract their claws, like cats, so as not to harm the singing baby nightingale—a figure for Mary Fairfax. It is men in George Wither's picture who bring down a great tree, and the woodpecker in Jacob Cats' emblem merely carves his nestinghole (fig. 3); there is no explanation in the poem of just how a woodpecker fells a great oak. Nor do we know from the poet why the supposedly contented doves should "mourn," nor why the heron (substituted in the poem for the canonical stork, rare in Yorkshire) should drop its first-born, as the stork does in Arnoldus Freitag's picture (fig. 4). As we work our way through relevant texts, we discover that all these birds, even the stork and the heron, are particularly distinguished for the care they take of their young—as the dove does just that in Alciato's emblem, or the stork feeds its young in mid-air as that little creature learns to fly (fig. 5). The halcyon, likened to Maria who stills the landscape where she has been, broods its nestlings on the quiet sea. Marvell's selection of creatures supports, then, a major theme of his poem, the duty parents owe their children—exemplified in the Fairfaxes' training of young Maria. But all this is latent in the image, rather than verbally developed: Marvell forces us to act like the readers of emblems, a form notoriously relying on diaeresis, on the actual and conceptual space around each of its elements, caption, figure, and epigram. *We* supply the connectives: *we* see why the adage applies to a given figure, what in an epigram supports the idea pointed to by figure and adage.

REPETE.
VI.

13

VERS.
VVLGAR.
NOn amet, aut diſcat duros tolerare labores,
Optati compos qui velit eſſe ſui.

POLYB. LIB. 10.

NVlla re utili abſtinendum eſt, propter apparentem difficultatem; ſed comparan-
dus habitus, quo cuncta bona mortalibus comprehenſibilia redduntur.

B 3

Buyten

Fig. 3. The woodpecker's persistence. Cats, *Silenus Alcibiadis*.
Courtesy Bodleian Library.

Further, such space between its elements may be seen as
necessary in a form relying on such different sorts of allusion,
as the emblem does. Its epigram insists on syntactical com-

Fig. 4. The stork sacrificing its young. Freitag, *Mythologia Ethica*. Copyright British Museum.

pression; its figure often seems to illustrate nothing at all without its verbal accompaniments to direct our thoughts to the "idea" lying behind this ensemble of parts.

This directive lies behind the structure of these images, I think: in one last example from Marvell's poem, let me show

Fig. 5. The stork feeding its young in mid-air. Camerarius, *Symbolorum et emblematum . . . centuriae.* Courtesy Bodleian Library.

how much—*multum*—can be gathered in little. Education is
one of the poem's themes; another, its apparent opposite, is
"home." That is, the poem deals with a base, a settlement, a
habitat, at the same time that it treats training, development,
emergence. What kind of home should a man have, from
which he should emerge? Related to this question is the topical theme of retirement and activity. Early in the poem, birds
in their nests occur as analogues to Fairfax on his Appleton
estate; another creature so mentioned is the tortoise, retiring,
sensitive, dwelling "In cases fit of tortoise-shell," which "fit"
the creature as Fairfax's house fits him. In Henry Peacham's
emblem book—and in Johannes Sambucus', Geoffrey Whit-
ney's, Wither's, and others—we can find the tortoise bearing
various themes of this poem—of retiredness (fig. 6), of domestic economy, of sufficiency, of virginity, of proper matron-
hood. In the poem's last stanza, as the night comes down on
the valley and the poem must end, the following is said to
occur:

> But now the Salmon-fishers moist
> Their Leathern Boats begin to hoist:
> And, like Antipodes in Shooes,
> Have shod their heads in their Canoos.
> How Tortoise-like, but not so slow,
> These rational Amphibii go?
> Let's in: for the dark Hemisphere
> Doth now, like one of them, appear.

Fishermen with boats on their heads (that look like huge
shoes) are, then, likened to men upside down—*Homo arbor
inversa*, with a difference (fig. 7). That is to say, like Anti-
podeans, a pun. The notion of the Antipodes trips us into the
notion of hemisphere, for half the sphere is "ours" and half
"theirs"—and, also, Renaissance cartographies associated the
two topics under one rubric. The fishermen coming from the

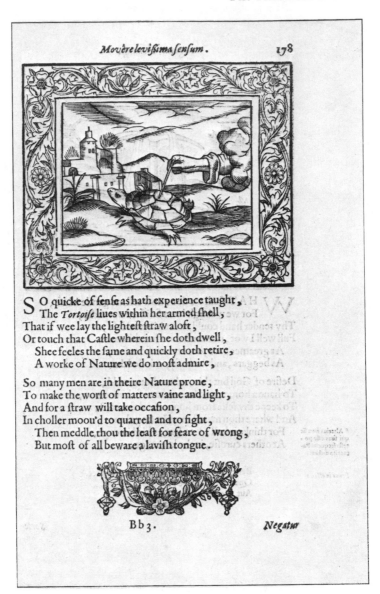

Fig. 6. The sensitive, retiring tortoise.
Peacham, *Minerva Brittanica*.

Fig. 7. Man as inverted tree. Jode, *Microcosmos.*
Copyright British Museum.

river are amphibious creatures, as is the tortoise, whose shell ("house") is hemispherical. The tortoise joins all these notions together, and by his inherent hemisphericity and houseness links them to the cupola'd Appleton House, real and symbolic locale of the poem. That the tortoise is also involved in retirement ("Let's in") and activity (Salmon-fishers), self-sufficiency and protection of matrons and virgins, sensibility and worldly wisdom, offers a shimmering, resonant set of meanings behind the already rich metaphorical and symbolic implications of the text's words. If this seems unlikely, then perhaps the figure from Zachiarias Heyn's emblembook, illustrating a piece of information got from Pliny and Diodorus Siculus, which shows the tortoise-shell as boat (activity) and as house (retirement), the housed man like the antipodean fisherman with boat on his head, may serve as a source for the translation of such a system of symbolic meanings into metaphor (fig. 8). But without all this attribution to the tortoise—and without our understanding of it—the image is merely unexpected, bizarre, a bit too smart. When we can supply something to back up the allusion, the text, already rich enough, increases manifold—in artistry.

By the simultaneous exactness of his imagery and his image's reverberations beyond the words written, Marvell incorporates something of the precision and the symbolic secrecy of the emblem form; by refusing to tell all and by making us work it out, he translates into poetry the theory of that eccentric and special kind.

In the work of another poet, George Herbert, I think emblem-theory makes a similar contribution, but to another end. The book of emblems was a collection, an anthology, which at first anyway did not present work in any serial or ordered fashion. Alciato called his book a "farrago": his subject or topic changed from emblem to emblem, and the reader was, therefore, called on to engage himself, work out a new puzzle, with each new emblem. As with adages, the elements of the emblem, of course, fit into many contexts—in any series of secular emblem books we come to recognize a picture which has migrated from context to context (often reversed in a new woodcut version), more often than not decorated with a new

Vivitur parvo bene.

7

Genefis.
18.5.

Ick wil u een bete broods geven , daer na fult ghy
voort gaen.

Ie t'apporteray vn morcheau de pain, puis apres vous
paßerez.

B b iij

Een

Fig. 8. The tortoise-shell as boat and as house. Heyns,
Emblemata.

caption or adage. That is, like adages, the elements of an emblem could be atomized and reformed in different contexts.

But not all emblem books were farragoes: gradually, specialities developed within the genre, thematic emblem books such as Otto van Veen's *Emblemata amatoria*, dependent upon the love-epigrams of the Anthology, *Emblemata Horatiana*, from Horace, and *Emblemata amoris divini*, in which the Eros and Anteros of the love-emblems were decorously haloed and clad as Amor Divinus and Anima (fig. 9). There were also books of political emblems, and emblems for women— as one can see, the emblem book was becoming less enigmatic, less puzzling, and was taking to didactic endeavors. It is with sacred emblems that I want to stay for my present subject: some of these, almost uniformly Roman Catholic emblem books, offered orderly devotional programs to their readers, as in Henry Hawkins', Hermannus Hugo's, and Benedictus Haeftanus' various books. Protestant religious emblem books tended still to a haphazardness which has to do, I think, with Protestantism—when Francis Quarles and Christopher Harvey used the cuts from Hugo and Haeftanus, for instance, they entirely broke up the sequences and altered the emphases of their sources to produce highly varied sets of emblems, in no particular progressive arrangement. I want to suggest that in George Herbert's collection of sacred poems, *The Temple*, can be found something of the emblem-technique of immediacy, as well as the mode of understanding we have watched Marvell exploiting. Although there are certainly grouped poems in *The Temple*—at the beginning, with "Church-porche," "Superliminarie," etc.; at the end, with the Four Last Things and a final eucharistic poem on Love; in clusters through the book (the emblematic poems on church architecture and appointments; the poems on Holy Week and Easter)—*The Temple* as a whole resists schemes to organize it into a consistent structure, although scholars

Fig. 9. Eros and Anteros transformed as Amor
Divinus and Anima. Hugo, *Pia Desideria*.

have tried to fit it to one or another Procrustean bed. Actually, I think this is deliberate: that Herbert, in good Protestant form, planned to call upon a reader's ever-revived capacity to contribute to his own revelation.

Let me run through a few of the ways in which emblem-theory and emblem-technique seem to me to help in this enterprise. Certainly Herbert's titles often relate to their poems as one part of the emblem does to another—as in the emblem, the connective leap must be made from title to poem and back again, as in the too-familiar poems "The Pulley," and "The Collar," which never mention things to do with their titles. One must catch on to the meanings, presented in mini-revelation. The well-known sonnet "Prayer" may do as a sample, a series of appositives, all of which lead to an experience of understanding—

> Prayer the Churches banquet, Angels age,
> Gods breath in man returning to his birth,
> The soul in paraphrase, heart in pilgrimage,
> The Christian plummet sounding heav'n and earth;
> Engine against th' Almightie, sinners towre,
> Reversed thunder, Christ-side-piercing spear,
> The six-daies world transposing in an houre,
> A kinde of tune, which all things heare and fear;
> Softnesse, and peace, and joy, and love, and blisse,
> Exalted Manna, gladnesse of the best,
> Heaven in ordinarie, man well drest,
> The milkie way, the bird of Paradise,
> Church-bels beyond the starres heard, the souls bloud,
> The land of spices; something understood.

Something understood—by the reader, by the praying man, by his deity: in this understatement, but only after having worked through the meaning of each phrase, the experience comes to be circumscribed and closed in by the experiencing reader, without any loss of transcendence; understanding comes, in part from the extraordinary diversity of the categories, like the peculiar juxtapositions in emblematic figures from which the phrases are drawn (fig. 10).

Though there are many more arguments for and examples of the emblematic in Herbert's technique, I want to look now at the poem "Hope," in which an exchange of gifts takes place between the human speaker and Hope—

> I gave to Hope a watch of mine: but he
>   An anchor gave to me.
> Then an old prayer-book did present:
>   And he an optick sent.
> With that I gave a vial full of tears:
>   But he a few green eares.
> Ah Loyterer! I'le no more, no more I'le bring:
>   I did expect a ring.

The exchange is carried on in emblematic language—the watch, the old book, the vial or glass of water are standard elements of the *Vanitas*, the still-life of transience. The anchor is a common emblem for hope, of course (fig. 11); in Hugo's and Quarles' emblem books, little Anima brings heaven nearer with a telescope or "optick." Paul's grain had been the subject of many emblems of the resurrection (fig. 12); Alciato himself commented on the greenness of that particular image for hope. But our little speaker, bringing the poor best he's got to the exchange, misunderstands the emblem-language in which he chose to woo Hope: by voicing his disappointment, he shows that he entirely misunderstood the nature of "hope," a condition, not a contract sealed by a ring.

I want to suggest that there is a major emblematic sub-theme in Herbert's Temple as a whole; that the collection is, among other things, a "school of the heart" much like con-

Fig. 10. Prayer. Hugo, *Pia Desideria*.

Mihi autem adhærere Deo bonum eſt , ponere in
Domino Deo ſpem meam. Pſalm. 72.

XXVIII.

Fig. 11. The anchor as symbol of hope. Hugo, *Pia Desideria*.

Fig. 12. A few green ears of grain as symbol of the Resurrection. Camerarius, Symbolorum et emblematum . . . centuriae. Courtesy Bodleian Library.

tinental devotional emblem books. The highly emblematic poem "Love-unknowne," long recognized as related to emblems, offers a good example of the emblematic heart-poem. Its speaker goes unenlightened from one peculiar experience to another, as his heart is thrown into a font, put in a cauldron that is in a furnace, tortured with thorns. There is no sign in the poem of what we soon come to expect in Roman Catholic "Schools of the Heart," of little Anima helping Divine Love blow the bellows for the flame (fig. 13); rather, in this poem, the heart so treated is made to seem utterly separate from the speaker, its ostensible possessor, who watches the strange signs as in a trance or dream. The pictures from Daniel Cramer's *Emblemata sacra* are more like the images in Herbert's poem—the heart detached, to suffer severely and alone. At the poem's end, the explanation for all this given by a listening "Friend" is as unequivocal as Cramar's emblems labelled "Probor" (fig. 14), "Non Laedor," "Mollesco" (fig. 15), and so on:

> The Font did onely, what was old, renew:
> The Caldron suppled, what was grown too hard:
> The Thorns did quicken, what was grown too dull. . . .

Old Petrarchan tortures of the heart, illustrated in a fifteenth-century woodcut by Meister Kaspar, have become sacramentalized in this tradition, much as love-language was made sacred by devotional poets, so that the "love" which causes these pains and purifies the heart is truly "unknowne" to the Christian undergoing his painful purification.

It is instructive to enumerate the various heart-images in Herbert's book: the heart has a mouth, "runs mutt'ring up and downe" ("A True Hymne"); it is busy and enquiring ("The Discharge"); it can spin; it is pressed and runs thin ("Praise III") (fig. 16); it is wrung out; it has hands ("The Collar"), knees ("The Deniall"), and feet ("A True

CORDIS PROBATIO

Fig. 13. Anima helping Amor Divinus refine the heart. Haeftanus,
Schola Cordis.

DECAS III.   109

EMBLEMA XXIV.
Elegi te in camino paupertatis.
Eſa. 48.10.
Ich wil dich außerwehlet machen im Ofen des Elendes.

PROBOR

XXIV.

Vrit & exercet Dominus nos igne camini:
Siu probus & conſtans, atque probandus eris.

REFRI-

Fig. 14. The heart refined. Cramer, *Emblemata Sacra.*
Copyright British Museum.

59

Fig. 15. The heart softened. Cramer, *Emblemata Sacra*.
Copyright British Museum.

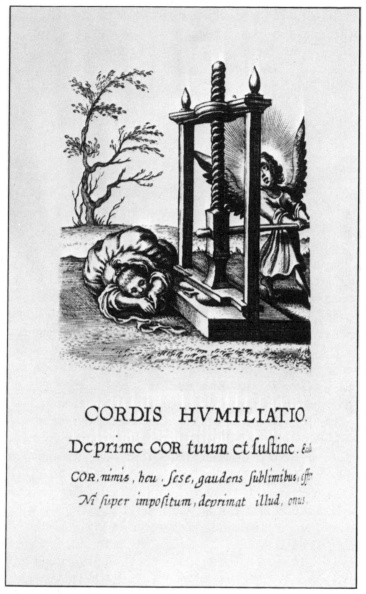

CORDIS HVMILIATIO.

Deprime COR tuum. et suftine. *ẽ:ũ*

COR. *nimis* , *heu* . *sese* , *gaudens fublimibus* , *eſſⁱ*
Ni fuper impoſitum , *deprimat illud* , *onus* .

Fig. 16. The heart pressed. Haeftanus, *Schola Cordis*.

Hymne"), like that odd picture in Haeftanus' *Schola Cordis*, where the heart reflected in a mirror sprouts two little hands and two little feet; it has eyes ("The Discharge," "Ephes. 4.30," "The Dawning") (fig. 17). It can sleep and rise, with and without the wings it often asks for. This heart is hard, sometimes softened, sometimes hardened by a hammer; it is cut by cords as in the *Schola Cordis*; its thoughts are as a case of knives wounding it, but it is relieved when "suppling grace" drops from above.

In several poems, the heart asks to be written on, or carved on as stone, most notably in the poem called "IESU" (fig. 18); the heart is "shrivel'd," but recovers greenness, as in the picture from Johann Mannich's book in which the heart sprouts grain afresh (fig. 19). God's "strong hand" (as in "Prayer II") works in some of Herbert's poems as it does characteristically in the emblems, where a mighty hand emerges from a cloud to do one or another remarkable thing —unlock the heart, as in "Church lock and key," or plumb heaven and earth or the human heart (fig. 20). God's hand or His voice intervenes in Herbert's poems of contract, to grant some favor ("Redemption") or to void a previous contract. His voice or His pen often rewrites one of Herbert's poems. This kind of imagery stresses, also, the unexpectedness, incalculability, and immediacy of spiritual experience, the mysteriousness of grace as well as its unmistakable importance to the Christian who must cope always with what he cannot yet quite understand.

As you can see, I think that both this immediacy and this incalculability derive from the psychological appeal of the emblem to its reader, inducing a set for solving problems. The kind of implied meaning noted in Marvell's tortoise-imagery in *Upon Appleton House*, where many things are drawn into a single hieroglyph, we may find paralleled in Herbert's very different equivalencies for the heart he educates in his book.

Fig. 17. The heart with eyes. Haeftanus, *Schola Cordis*.

DECAS III. 103

EMBLEMA XXIII.

Ille vocabit in nomine Iacob, & hic fcribet manu fua Domino.

Efa. 44.5.

Jener wird genennet werden mit dem Namen Jacob. Und dieser wird sich mit seiner Hand dem HErren zuschreiben.

PRÆDESTINOR

XXIII.

Annumeror Chriflo, cui fum de nomine notus,
Rubrica is vita eft penna liberque mee.

G 5 PRO·

Fig. 18. The heart written upon. Cramer, *Emblemata Sacra.*
Copyright British Museum.

Fig. 19. The heart sprouting grain afresh. Mannich,
Sacra Emblemata.

122

XXXIV.

Maer ons heeft Godt gheopenbaert door synen Geest; Want de Geest ondersoeckt alle dingh, oock de diepten Godts: Want vvat Mensche vveet, vvat in den Mensche is, dan de Geest des Menschen, die in den Mensche is, 1.Cor.2.10.11. & v.15.16. *de Geestelycke Mensche,&c. Wie cant' Herte doorgronden: Ick de Heere bent, die,&c.* Jer.17.9.

Ondersoeckt u selven, beproeft u selven, of ghy in den Gheloove syt, ofte niet: Weet ghy niet, dat Christus in u is? 2.Cor.13.

Godts Sin syn Geest ons openbaert:
Doorsoeckt dan hoe u herte vaert.

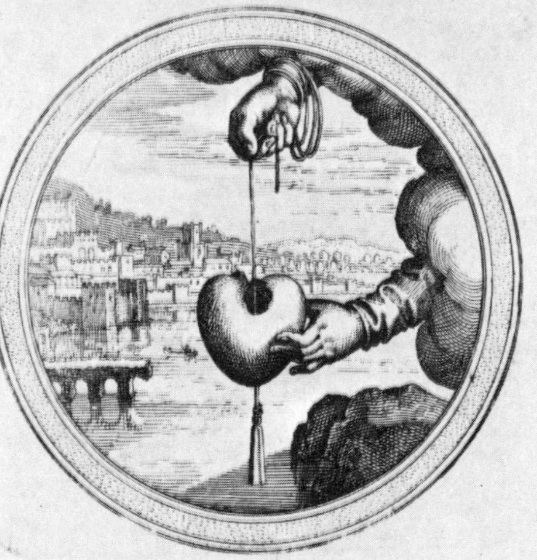

Rom.11. 34. Hoe comt de Mensch daer aen' van Godes Sin te kennen?
Hoe can hy seker zyn van syne saligheyt?
1.Cor.2.15. 16. Hoe comt syn hert gerust, wie heeft hem sulcks geseyt?
Dat s' t' vraeghen van die gen, die dese Leer ontkennen.

Arm

Fig. 20. The heart plumbed by God's hand. Heinsius, *Emblemata Amatoria*. Copyright British Museum.

The true temple of God is not a temple, but the human heart —for all its architectural poems, Herbert's book *The Temple* is written out of and for that metaphor: it is a school for the heart, teaching it to become a temple fit for God's dwelling.

These examples are of the comfortable interaction of one poetic kind, understood in its specialness, the emblem, upon another, more open kind, the devotional lyric. These may stand as examples of genres fronting on one another, sharing their specialness in a common mode. I want to talk a little about another sort of interchange between two other short-form kinds, epigram and sonnet, which we might think of as countergenres—twinned and yet opposite. Though definitions of "epigram" vary considerably in our period, we may take the epigram to be a poem no shorter than a distich, and (so long as the Martial was regarded as the primary epigrammatist) pithy, sharp, often dealing with various social and occupational foibles. An epigram might be epideictic (praise of a ruler, a hero, a servant); it might be an epitaph; it might celebrate a public event, a victory, a great building, a significant person living or dead. Depending on its subject or topic, it might use a variety of styles—

> Underneath this sable hearse
> Lies the subject of all verse . . .
>
> In this little Urne is laid
> Prewdence Baldwin (once my Maid) . . . .

In tone, the epigram could range from celebration to insult, its topic from emperor to prostitute, its style from high to low. But it must be brief, according to ancient practitioners and modern theorists; its inherent terseness—*brevita*—was regarded as the result of its origin in incised inscription. The epigram was, of course, the chief literary form for much in little—cf. Herrick's *tours-de force* or Angelus Silesius' highly paradoxical compressions of the mysteries of theological doctrine and the ineffability of deity.

With the recovery of the Greek *Anthology,* printed by Estienne with a careful introductory essay, a "sweet" or amorous epigram was revealed in multitudinous variation. By the time Scaliger, my peculiar hero, published his *Poetices* in 1561, he was able to classify the emblematic types in a series of metaphorical larder-terms. Epigrams, he said, could be stinking and foul, but this type was beneath the notice of serious poets or critics. The important categories for epigram were *fel* (gall), *acetum* (vinegar), *sal* (salt), and *mel* (honey). Against this schematization, we can understand Robortello's view that the epigrams were miniature versions of greater kinds —epitaphs of tragedy, epideictic epigrams of odes, bitter epigrams of satire, and vinegar and salt epigrams of comedy. As a result of the mass of *mel*-epigrams in the *Anthology*—poems about Cupid and his bow, his bee, his lions, etc., these literary sources for *Emblemata amatoria*—genre-critics in the Renaissance scurried to find a Roman equivalent for the type, as well as a modern equivalent. They came up with Catullus as the Latin analogue (a regular topic for criticism was the *paragone* of Martial and Catullus as the best epigrammatist), and with the sonnet as the equivalent of this kind of epigram in modern times—Petrarca was the usual example in Italy, Scève, Sainte-Marthe, and later Ronsard in France. Some theorists made plain their opinion that epigram and sonnet were closely connected (Varchi, Pigna, Tasso); others that they were parallel but entirely different thematic genres (Minturno). In both his theoretical statements and his practice Du Bellay linked the two; Vauquelin de la Fresnaye said of him,

> Et Du Bellay quitant cette amoureuse flame,
> Premier fist le Sonet sentir son Epigramme. . . .

Small Forms: Multo in Parvo

Du Bellay certainly played with the condiments listed by Scaliger—in his famous "J'ay oublié l'art de petrarquizer," he wrote of ladies' sweetness as "sucre et miel," of her rigours as "aloës et fiel"; in the Latin epigram "Ad Lectorem" heading his remarkable sonnet-sequence *Les Regrets*, Du Bellay promised a book mixing gall, honey, and salt.

In *Les Regrets*, Du Bellay wrote sonnets nostalgic, critical, personal: public sonnets about public life, public men, public events, even public buildings. Some praised a few virtuous men he knew in Rome, many more were diatribes against wicked men and wicked customs. We can recognize Du Bellay's reliance upon Martial and Juvenal for similar attacks upon Roman *mores*, and we can detect his epigraphical awareness in his sonnets on the buildings of ancient Rome crumbling before his eyes. There is relatively little "honey" or love-matter in this important sequence, but *sal* and *fel* are not lacking. In English, we find many uses of "sweet," "honey," "sugar" and "salt" as metaphors for style and for substance—as metaphors for the behavior, for instance, of mistress to lover in a typical sonnet-sequence. In this sense, the Princess of France plays with "honey" and "gall," "sweet" and "bitter" in her exchange with Berowne in *Love's Labour's Lost*, as Samuel Daniel does also in his *Delia*. If one combines the two areas, then one would expect that of a loving lover the poet properly writes sonnets, of an unloving lover epigrams.

You can see what the next sentence is going to be: I suggest that this is exactly what Shakespeare did in his remarkable sonnets. He played off not only kinds of love against one another, but also stylistic and generic milieux against one another. For a beloved typically more elevated than the poet, remote, cool, beautiful, kind but distant, he composed sonnets with all the *mel*, mellifluousness, of the Petrarchan convention —by his time, of course, grown sweeter than Petrarca ever allowed. Edward Hubler and others have noted how often the word "sweet" occurs in the sonnets to the young man; images of sweetness abound too—flowers, perfume, honey, springtime, and so on. These are, of course, clichés in the sonneteering business: Shakespeare's radicalism lies in his applying these epithets and metaphors to the love he bears a young man, not, as in the customary formula, to a mistress. Indeed, in literary type we can find few precedents for this sort of relation, though sonnet-mistresses were customarily icily detached, like this friend; whimsical in their attentions to poet-lover, like this friend; and even figuratively unfaithful—that is, favoring another over the poet, as this friend does. Much is transferred from the psychological situation, as well as the language, of petrarchist sonneteering to this odd set of sonnets; even the episode with the rival poet, original though it is in so many ways, can be seen as a transposition of the canonical rival lover.

In the images of sweetness, too, we may note that Shakespeare finds and exploits a figure for sweetness redoubled, the figure of distillation ("summer's distillation . . . / A liquid prisoner pent in walls of glass"; "Make sweet some vial") finally shifted from the lover to the poetry which is the container (walls of glass) for his particular sweetness:

> And so of you, beauteous and lovely youth,
> When that shall vade, by verse distills your truth.

But the young man is not all sweetness, as we learn from sonnets placed later in the series; first of all, slander slurs his beauty ("canker vice the sweetest buds doth love"); second, he deserves the slander—"O in what sweets dost thou thy sins enclose!" In this sonnet, Number 95, there is a remarkable balance between the language of *mel* and the language of something else—*acetum*, at least. In the first line, "sweet" and "lovely" meet with "shame"; in the second, "canker" concurs with "rose"; in the third, spot-beauty-budding; in the fourth, sweet-sins—and so on, through dispraise-praise, blesses-ill, vices-beauty's veil, blot-fair, so that when we reach the epigrammatic couplet, with its vocabulary of sharpness, we are at once readied and unready for its decisive summing up:

> Take heed, dear heart, of this large privilege;
> The hardest knife ill-us'd doth lose his edge.

I chose this sonnet because it has not been explicated unduly; its predecessor, Sonnet 94, "They that have power to hurt and will do none," actually says what I am fumbling for more succinctly as well as, of course, more beautifully. In this poem, the enigmatic nature of the praise puts us off: evidently the subject is being praised for the cool and courteous hypocrisy of a man unwarmed by ordinary human fires. The primary sonnet-language of "The summer's flow'r is to the summer sweet" is set off against a different image, involving a different vocabulary of associations: "But if that flow'r with base infection meet, / The basest weed outbraves his dignity." "Base infection," "basest weed" belong to another less flowery social world—to remind us, willy nilly, of the sonnets about the young man's low company. The final couplet, though, an epigram in itself, suits a commonplace metaphor to a particular situation at the same time that it calls into play opposing generic languages:

> For sweetest things turns sourest by their deeds:
> Lilies that fester smell far worse than weeds.

In the sonnets to the mistress, however, we find the language of epigram exploited more fully. In itself, this is another kind of inversion, since a sonnet-mistress is habitually treated with the humble and exasperated respect Shakespeare accords the young man in the early sonnets. Still, there are analogues to speaking about a mistress as Shakespeare does, from Catullus' magnificently compressed outbursts to such lesser examples as Sir John Davies' "Gulling Sonnets." In his *Contr'amours*, Etienne Jodelle had complained of his having convention-alized his mistress, gilded her dark locks worthy of Medusa, planing out the lines of her forehead, likening her thick eye-brows to Cupid's bow. Like Shakespeare in his fine anti-Petrarchan Sonnet 130, "My mistress' eyes are nothing like the sun," Jodelle acknowledged that his mistress when she walked also trod on the ground and that he, for all her un-conventional looks and his conventional patching of them, suffered for loving her as conventional lovers suffered from conventionally greater beauties.

If this be vinegar, Shakespeare is capable in the sonnets also of that gall and *foeditas*, stinkingness, which Scaliger for-bade the true poet. The "nothing" sonnets play upon the sexual sense of that word, its association with the female genitalia; and much in these poems reminds us of classical epigrams on prostitutes—the quantification, the attribution of accounting to the lady, the not-very circumlocution for the pudenda, the hint of physical geography we know from Mar-tial's epigrams. The lady's voracious sexuality is implied—in these poems (135–136), the poet good-humoredly accepts this state of things, and recognizes also the force of his own desire: if she will take him, even for a while, that is enough.

In 137, "Thou blind fool, Love, what dost thou to mine eyes / That they behold, and see not what they see?" the poet plays off various commonplaces from the petrarchan tradition of idealized love against the language of gall. Love enters the lover by his eyes to take control of his whole self; the lover is likened to a ship; the poet is concerned with "truth"—

> If eyes, corrupt by over-partial looks,
> Be anchor'd in the bay where all men ride,
> Why of eyes' falsehood hast thou forged hooks,
> Whereto the judgment of my heart is tied?

> Why should my heart think that a several plot,
> Which my heart knows the wide world's
>   common place?

Her corruption could not be more plainly stated—she is "the bay where all men ride" in a particularly repugnant sexual reference; "the wide world's common place."

At this point one may say, and rightly, that although the poet is writing about a mistress wrongly strayed into the sonnet-decorum in the language of another kind, yet he conforms even in this to the fundamental enterprise of sonneteering—namely, the exploration of emotional complexity for which sonnets so long provided the chief opportunity. Perhaps that is the force of a sonnet like 129, facing unflinchingly the realities of sexual love and recognizing that it is one's inmost judgment that establishes the value of this, or any other experience:

> Th'expense of spirit in a waste of shame
> Is lust in action; and till action, lust
> Is perjur'd, murd'rous, bloody, full of blame,
> Savage, extreme, rude, cruel, not to trust;
> Enjoy'd no sooner but despised straight;
> Past reason hunted, and, no sooner had,
> Past reason hated, as a swallowed bait,
> On purpose laid to make the taker mad—
> Mad in pursuit, and in possession so;
> Had, having, and in quest to have, extreme;
> A bliss in proof, and prov'd, a very woe;
> Before, a joy propos'd, behind, a dream.
>   All this the world well knows, yet none knows well
>   To shun that heaven that leads men to this hell.

This is a definition-poem which faces the excruciations of obsession, recognizing also that the heaven and hell of love are the poet's own internal states projected—"Why, this is hell, nor am I out of it."

But the poet *does* get out of it: in his difficulties with the young man, he had faced his own emotionalism about his friend's faults:

> All men make faults, and even I in this,
> Authorizing thy trespass with compare,
> Myself corrupting, salving thy amiss,
> Excusing thy sins more than thy sins are. . . .
>
> (35)

As he had learnt to put up with the friend's inconstancy, he now learns to put up with the lady's:

> So shall I live, supposing thou art true,
> Like a deceivèd husband
>
> (93)

> But what's so blessed-fair that needs no blot?
> Thou may'st be false, and yet I know it not.
>
> (92)

And, most wonderfully,

> When my love swears that she is made of truth,
> I do believe her, though I know she lies. . .
> Therefore I lie with her, and she with me,
> And in our faults by lies we flattered be.
>
> (138)

"Let me excuse thee," he says in the next sonnet; and later

> Why of two oaths' breach do I accuse thee,
> When I break twenty?
>
> (152)

Such self-knowledge owes something to one kind, the sonnet, but I shall not pretend that such self-acceptance owes to any: what I shall aver about these remarkable sonnets is that part of their power comes from the poet's capacity to enliven generic styles, to animate, confront, and intertwine lyric and epigrammatic styles in such a way as to permit the poet-figure in the poems a different kind of self-analysis from that of the sonnet genre, to permit him, indeed, to find another kind of self. The middle style between the high vocabulary of the love-sonnet and the low vocabulary of the epigram brackets a psychological and social reality between these two generic renderings of milieu. To borrow from another poet, John Harington, for a moment, whose epigram comparing the sonnet and the epigram ends,

> Well, though I grant Sugar may please the taste,
> Yet let my verse have salt to make it last.

I would suggest that, although Shakespeare trusted the sonnet-distillations to preserve his passion, for him both the banquet of *agape* and the sensual feast were heightened and refined by a pinch of salt. Or, to alter the metaphor slightly, with honey and salt, the styles and attitudes of sonneteer and epigrammatist, he could preserve the mixed bitter and sweet experience of loving, in a solution entirely his own.

III

Inclusionism: Uncanonical Forms, Mixed Kinds, and Nova reperta

In any discussion of mixed forms, especially mixed forms which are also uncanonical, disorganization tends to set in: I apologize at once for the discontinuities in this chapter. Its subject is the various uncanonical literary forms and subjects outside strict professional definitions of poetry, which fail to live up or down to generic regulation. In particular, I want to circle around the subject of literary and generic experimentation by mixing kinds, and by following out generic implications into new areas of expression. Aristotle's and Horace's rules for feigning, fiction, and poetry ruled out many of those dignified literary forms beloved of the humanists—the dialogue, the discourse, instructional treatises, utopias, and the like, thus setting up bounds beyond which proper literature should not pass. In Sidney's synoptic *Defense of Poesie*, we have noticed both the exclusionist view of literature as an art or craft, and the inclusionist view of literature as not only representing but as indeed being the *paideia*. More important even than this, we have noticed Sidney working from these two positions without acknowledging, or needing to acknowledge, the least conflict between them.

Certainly as far as *writers* were concerned, rules were there to take or leave—the Renaissance is rich in uncanonical kinds. Many examples of these works are so well written that we find ourselves, as scholars coming so long after, accepting the dialogue, the history, the philosophical poem, to say nothing of prose fictions, as "literature," and studying them with as much care as we do more officially "literary" works. The phenomenon of Rabelais is a case in point: there was no doubt that his lengthening book was a masterpiece and that everyone read it. Du Bellay referred to it in a sonnet about his journey home through Switzerland, calling the Swiss "Saul-cisses," as Rabelais had; Ronsard composed a comic-heroic epitaph on Rabelais, which clearly showed that he knew his book very well; but *Gargantua et Pantagruel* does not appear in any discussion of poetry, or imaginative literature, in the period.

Not that it is an easy book to talk about—obviously it is a comic-ironic fiction, with an immense scope of allusion to—and thus recollection of—the matter and forms of literature and of the intellectual life. I suppose Northrop Frye's definition, "anatomy," is as good as any for this very mixed book, though it makes me a trifle nervous: in any case, Rabelais surely displays that intellectual view of the world that Frye postulates as necessary for this category. One can say, *avant la lettre*, that Rabelais was concerned with semiotic systems, for which he took languages—naturally—as his metaphors and examples. Merely in the way he manages the languages of countries, provinces, professions, trades, social classes, and even of sexes, we can see Rabelais' extraordinary interest in the variety of modes of thought in his world, as well as his powerful drive to get "everything" in, so as to make his book represent and comment on culture. Herman Meyer has written about literary quotation—really, about literary allusion—in this book; Rabelais exploits the power and variety of allusion as shortcuts to categorization. His parodies of pettifoggery are in themselves comic, but they do more than amuse. Quotations from the *legistes*' style (ff. De suis et legit.,

i. Intestato par. fi.; Gallus, ff. De lib. et posthu., et l. septimo ff. De stat. homi.) demonstrate both the limitations and the totality of a language-system: an interpretation of the world may be absolute in its own terms, but the terms are glaringly partial. In other applications of this trick, Rabelais at once exposes and confirms human systems—in his genealogies, his parodied library-catalogues, his get-wise-quick citations from Erasmus' *Adagia*, he reveals the limitations of even very large categories. He mimics the humanist education which takes its natural history from Pliny, Dioscorides, and Aelian, its hunting and fishing from Oppian and Julius Pollux, its agriculture from Cato, Varro, Columella, and Vergil; he mocks the new form of utopia while praising the concept it formulates. With his parodies of that most cherished of humanist arts, letter-writing, and his paradoxical encomia of this and that, we sense the sharp commentary on the fakeries and chinks in the humanist program—but when we compare his attacks on these things with his attitude to scholastic learning, it is clear where his sympathies lie. For all his skepticism of the new learning, he supports it against the old.

In literary ways, Rabelais is remarkably eclectic: his awareness of medievalism emerges in his revival of Monsieur François Villon, Maître Pathelin, and le Franc Archer de Baignolet in hell, and he fits into his narrative the interpolated fabliaux and kyrielles of medieval convention. Of course these kyrielles —lists, catalogues—are a way of honoring the *genus universum*, of getting it all in, as well as of mocking epic catalogues. One might even say of this book that the many genres it comprises, from folk-tale through the *faux-naif* forms of medieval authors to "modern" versions of ancient forms, are all metaphorized for their thematic meanings and implications: what mimesis of reality there is lies in the author's attitude to the world, not in its mimetic reproduction, no matter what Auerbach has said of it. For it is the *structures* of literary form that are stressed by mockery in this formal style, as books and traditions of books are disposed to make moral points about human behavior and human culture. Like other books which therefore seem something like it—is this a genre, then? must I call it anatomy?—*Gargantua et Pantagruel* is a book of books, and of all kinds of books, so that for instance Pantagruel can be transformed from a little morality-devil who throws salt in men's mouths to make them thirsty, into a mighty humanist giant philosopher-king who travels the world to understand it all—and who can understand, among other things, why men drink prodigiously.

Though we cannot fail to notice the generic lowerings, the ironic mockery, of this book, we have to consider too how much this fantastic narrative is made up of extraliterary, even subliterary forms: the voyage, the oration, the debate, the utopia, the letter, some very new forms or forms newly established. It draws too on subliterary imaginative forms which it self-consciously elevates, sometimes by the dubious device of gigantism—folk-tale, fabulous story, morality, and fabliau are dignified by incorporation here. Mikhail Bakhtin may not be as right as one would wish about the book's owing its strength to popular forms, since most of these "popular" forms have survived by virtue of monkish script, but he *is* right to point to the very different decorums from which Rabelais drew, largely from uncanonical generic resources.

Similarly, Burton's *Anatomy of Melancholy* draws on a varied range of models and resources; I shall not dwell on this work for long, having worn myself out on it elsewhere. Suffice it to say that once more there is the conscious effort to gather into one book the possibilities of the intellectual world: medical, spiritual, and practical information, hearsay, folklore, fairy-tale all go in, sources quoted each time. Like the *Adagia* from which it pillaged so liberally, the *Anatomy* gives us our data for checking up on its whimsical, imaginative, impressionistic and canny author. Here again, we find sketches of forms (many of which are deliberately disavowed, such as the list in the introduction—pasquil, satire, paradox, etc.). Character, utopia, love-treatise, sermon, consolation, cosmic voyage are all somehow worked into this medical treatise, as are folk-forms—vulgar errors cited from Pliny, Athenaeus, or Burton's mother indiscriminately, fabliaux so gross that they could not be written down in English. As with Rabelais, Burton uses the kinds distinguished for the shape of their content, and, as also with Rabelais, for all his prolixity and prodigality, he was capable of remarkable compressions of all these things —his consolation, voyage, sermon, utopia, etc. are short versions of the real kinds. That is, he offers us a *florilegium*, an anthology of his own making (Democritus Junior!), and an anthology which, somehow, covers "everything" in the natural and conceptual world.

By means of these other genres, thematically and intellectually punctuating, counterpointing, heightening his discourse even when they seem most digressive within it, Burton managed to raise the genre of medical treatise to something literarily more honorable. His generic allusiveness permitted him to reconstruct by his own means (Democritus Junior once more) and to his own taste his intellectual cosmos. Of course there were literary precedents in antiquity, most of them quoted throughout the book—Aulus Gellius and other compendiarists, Athenaeus, Macrobius, Pliny, Aelian, Strabo, Philostratus, Apollodorus, together with those writers of what we now call anthological or anatomical fiction, Heliodorus, Petronius, Apuleius. Modern equivalents are cited too—Mateo Alemán's picaresque *Guzman de Alfarache*, *Don Quixote*, and again and again Rabelais. Burton's chief means of working in these cultural topics was in-formal, or antiformal: the digression. We have digressions on anatomy; on the nature of spirits, bad angels, and devils; on the miseries of scholars; on air (i.e., meteorology and cosmology); a consolatory digression; and anecdotal digressions untitled as such—or, we have speculative and critical essays detached from the carefully constructed diagram of the book's fundamental organization. Although most people derided the digression as a form, however much they may have enjoyed digressive authors, digressions have an unexpected defender in the scrupulously non-digressive Galileo Galilei, who likened them to the condiments and spices adorning the main food of a meal, as well as to the beautiful dishes and cups in which food and drink were served. Galileo was thinking of Ariosto, I suspect, for he located the majesty of heroic poetry in the variety and ease of its episodes; but the book he was specifically commenting on, Fortunatus Liceti's *Litheosporus*, belonged in fact to the kind of Burton's *Anatomy*, a book attempting systematic treatment of a scientific subject. Though he criticized the inaccuracy of its science in his *Sidereus Nuntius*, Galileo nonetheless valued its "mille e mille notizie" on all sorts of interesting topics. If one were pressed to find a model for Burton, I think one could do worse than light on Athenaeus' *Deipnosophists* (translated by some donnish wag as "the Gastronomers"). That extremely mixed collection of digressive and miscellaneous but hardly haphazard elements is, like the *Anatomy*, controlled by a masterful allusiveness to other forms, and is at the same time a member of a specific kind, the cookbook. Athenaeus' Symposium, his *Cena*, is a critical compendium of culture and theory of culture no less than its modern descendent, Lévi Strauss' *Le cru et le cuit*.

For all their gusto and magnitude, their fullness and thickness, Rabelais' and Burton's books bear more likeness to Erasmus' *Adagia* than just their unstinting use of its contents—like it, they are "centos," books of quotation and allusion, on a very large scale, to all the conceivable elements of their culture. Though they mix the categories by which aspects of culture are usually communicated, they nonetheless recognize those categories as the scaffolding for their own constructions. The last section of Burton's book, an endless discussion of love-melancholy and religious melancholy, is topically organized along the lines of any Neoplatonic love-dialogue—a bit blasphemous, since the "melancholies" so subvert the absolute values of both. By this arrangement, though, Burton acknowledged a conventional hierarchy of values even as he questioned it in general and in its particulars by pointing out the dysfunctional aspects of its notions of love. Generic organization is treated dialectically in this sense: the organization itself provides one-half the argument. A clearer example of this is to be found in Montaigne's "Apologie," where the general structure of Sebonde's argument, on which Montaigne arranges his refutations, becomes the author's silent antagonist.

In both Rabelais' and Burton's books, the principal kinds exploited are non-poetic: they carry an early humanist preoccupation into a later age, insisting on elevating to belletristic status kinds which had slipped below the level of artistic attention. In the literature of the late Renaissance there are many samples of such elevation—a recent article on Donne's *Devotions upon Emergent Occasions* by Jonathan Goldberg shows how it exploits and intensifies the clearly subliterary devotional books on spiritual sickness; Louis Martz' and now Barbara Lewalski's studies of very different generic forms of meditation have shown us how this subliterary genre affected major poetry in the seventeenth century; we are beginning to understand how much more nearly "Compleat" Izaak Walton's book is than just a treatise on angling; work on dialogue and debate opens up its capacities for enriching many different belletristic works—*Love's Labours Lost* and *Paradise Regain'd* being only the most obvious.

Perhaps consideration of the ways of highly formal but not-quite-literary kinds may slightly alter our conception of the functions of certain of Sir Thomas Browne's works, even to smoothing out a conflict in his utterance which has bothered some of his most devoted admirers. In his *Pseudodoxia Epidemica*, a lengthy corrective to popular errors such as the belief that "a Bear brings forth her young informous and unshapen, which she fashioneth after by licking them over"; or "that the roots of the Mandrakes do make a noise, or give a shriek upon eradication"; or "that Men weigh heavier dead than alive," Browne specifically denies some of the methodological principles which he took as fundamental to later masterpieces, *The Garden of Cyrus* and *Urne-Buriall*. In the *Pseudodoxia*, he condemned outright "the Hieroglyphical Doctrine of the Ægyptians" as having much advanced "many popular conceits. For using an Alphabet of Things, and not of words, through the image and pictures thereof, they endeavored to speak their hidden conceits in the letters and language of Nature." This is, of course, the fundamental technique of *The Garden of Cyrus*, where "the Hieroglyphics of the brazen table of Bembus," the hieroglyphical language of "the mysticall Statua of Janus," and, indeed, the hieroglyphical language of the Creator Himself in forming things by fives and in five-sided shapes, are taken for granted as signs of order in a multitudinous, varied, fragmented creation difficult to organize conceptually. Must we say, as one of my professors used to, that Browne regressed methodologically as he grew older, declining from modern empiricism to old-fashioned mysticism, or may we look for another reason, a more literary cause, for so singular a methodological contradiction in the works of a man manifestly concerned throughout his life with method?

To begin with the later works, *Hydriotaphia, or Urne-buriall* and *The Garden of Cyrus, or the Quincuncial Lozenge, or Net-work Plantations of the Ancients, Artificially, Natural-*

ly, Mystically Considered, are organized alike, each book with
five sections ("the quincunx artificially consider'd") which
can be seen to match one another. Frank Huntley, the clever-
est student so far of these works, has shown how they dovetail
into each other until in fact they form a single work made
of two mirroring parts. At first glance, though, this is not apparent: *Urne-buriall* is an occasional work on the finding of
some bone-filled urns not far from where Browne lived; *The
Garden of Cyrus* is a meditative discourse on the symbolic
effects and meanings of gardening. Both, one might note at
once, are in proper humanist, if improper belletristic genres,
the one depending heavily on the archaeological treatise, the
other on the georgic tradition. Browne's study of burial customs over the known world offers us an insight into the state
of archaeology and anthropology at that time; it ends with
a meditation upon the meaning of Christian burial and the
hope of the life to come. *The Garden of Cyrus* has no such
specific occasion: it deals with plantations and plants (artificial
and natural creations), its jumping-off place being the first
garden rather than the hanging gardens of Babylon, which
are merely touched upon in their historical place. According
to Zenophon, Cyrus' trees were set in groups of five, a planting
practice recorded also by Varro. Browne turns this shape into
a schematic cross—X, T, .:. , and proceeds from this
figure to deduce everything in nature and the arts and crafts,
proving to his satisfaction the proposition he stated in the
Religio Medici, that "Nature is the art of God." Quincuncial
forms were, he found, set on every sort of thing—the scales
of beavers' tails, the shape of seedpods, the military order of
Greeks and Persians, plantations by all people, in all places,
at all times. The material for this treatise, as the material for
the *Urne-Buriall,* points to many different topics developed
more systematically in other works—archaeology, architecture,
military arts, agriculture and horticulture, geography, cosmol-

ogy, history, theology, and theogony, natural history, even biography. The material on crosses, for example, comes from Lipsius' archaeological study of that subject, *De Cruce*, one illustration of which provided Donne with many of his odd and refreshing examples of ubiquitous crosses in his poetic meditation in this kind, "The Crosse." Cato, Columella and Varro reliably produce many of Browne's examples of planting; Aeneas Tacticus and Vegetius' *De re militaria* offered examples of military order; Dioscorides, Conrad Gesner, Charles de l'Ecluse, Thomas Mouffet, Casper Bauhin and other naturalists and herbalists provided the natural-historical quincunxes.

Urne-Buriall naturally exploits archaeological literature, especially that on sepulchral customs—Lilius Gregorius Gyraldi's study of ancient interment, Antonio Bosio's wonderful *Roma sotterranea*, Jean-Jacques Chifflet's account of Frankish burials, and several others. Browne's essays work in the encyclopedic mode, but miniature, symbolically: here everything stands for something else, and any specific thing is through its symbolic implications connected with everything else. While working in one category, Browne shows that all other categories can be involved in any single one. These essays are epitomes of the intellectual as of the natural world; further, in their interrelation with each other, the two works demonstrate the conceptual method with magisterial finality, as their apparent systematic differences fuse to provide an anatomy of the world. The creation, creatures, and creativity are all seen under the aspect of eternity. Life is death, as death is life—"To live indeed is to be again our selves, which being not an hope but an evidence in noble believers; 'Tis all one to lye in St. Innocents Church-yard, as in the Sands of Ægypt: ready to be anything, in the extasie of being ever, and as content with six feet as the Moles of Adrianus," is the last sentence of *Urne-Buriall*. This of *The Garden of Cyrus*:

"But who can be drowsie at that howr which freed us from everlasting sleep? Or have slumbring thoughts at that time, when sleep it self must end, and as some conjecture all shall wake again?" The question opens upon vistas of vast eternity.

In Rabelais' and Burton's books we have seen the "cento" method, the method of categorical selection, which allows an author to treat existing knowledge as if for his own sake, that he might find his particular way of understanding "everything," of comprehending everything in his own intellectual creation. Browne treats the body of learning and the body of nature as Erasmus had treated ancient texts, aphoristically: meanings are compressed into the scale of a fish or a seedpod, and these are arranged to suit Browne's particular vision of the universe. Aphoristically, then, but also metaphorically: the kinds themselves become metaphorical, to be disposed as figures are disposed, at the writer's will.

To say this another way, Browne worked to reestablish thematic genres—archaeology, geography, history, and the like—genres which would have seemed fully literary to Petrarca and Boccaccio, as well as to the humanists of the *quattrocento*; and to restore to them their lost status as literature. But though he has relied on these humanistic genres for his matter, he uses them all the same as generic allusions or as generic structures adapted to *his* form, a new essayistic form—old bodies in new urns, *nova reperta*, new uses of old forms, seen in a new context. Other new forms helped him in this effort—the essay, so long unrecognized as a literary genre although practiced as if it were; the meditation upon the creatures in which he innovates considerably.

To return to the *Pseudodoxia*, we recognize that this work, seeking to eradicate intellectual error, was manifestly in the tradition of Bacon and other moderns trying to clear the underbrush in the way of a new vision of truth. The fact that Browne's effort seems as quaint and superstitious to us as do those authors who seemed superstitious to him illustrates the great dilemma in any such enterprise: Bacon's *Sylva Sylvarum,* another work designed to set practical experimentation on a sound basis by offering correctives to received opinion, was, if anything, even fuller of misapprehensions than this book of Browne's. Giambattista Della Porta, in his *Naturall Magic,* Girolamo Cardano in *De Subtilitate* sought like Browne to reform information on a very broad scale; that Scaliger heartlessly attacked Cardano's book in his own *Esoteric Exercises* (corrected in its turn by many subsequent readers) simply offers the most graphic example of the problem of this genre. For the very authors Browne found most culpable in promulgating and preserving vulgar errors—Pliny, Diodorus Siculus, Athenaeus, Isidore of Seville, Bartholomaeus Anglicus, and other late-classical and medieval encyclopedists—are responsible both for his method, which their kinds of error dictate, and for his form. For years I could not understand why Browne included a whole book on iconographical errors, until it finally dawned on me that this was a Plinian category honored precisely because painting was an important topic in the *Natural History.* Browne knows the proper audience-response to Pliny or Athenaeus, whom he called "a most delectable author, very various . . . Being miscellaneous in many things, he is to be received with suspition; for such as amass all relations, must erre in some, and may without offence be unbelieved in many." So of himself: "Thus, I say, must these authors be read, and thus must we be read our selves for discoursing of matters dubious, and many controvertible truths; we cannot without arrogancy entreat a credulitie, or implore any farther assent, then the probabilitie of our Reason, and verity of experiments induce." Skepticism, then, is written into this genre, just as faith is written into the mode of meditation; in other words, from Browne we can learn that the miscellaneous and wonderful materials of the natural world and the world of thought can be organized into *different* encyclopedic forms, one, the *Pseudodoxia*, in the low style of modest inquirer after truth, another in the high style of vatic interpreter of nature.

Perhaps I may turn to Browne's masterwork, the *Religio Medici*, both to round out one version of an ancient genre-system by producing a work in the middle style, and also to stress a problem I have insufficiently touched on, the invention or the finding of new forms—the literary *nova reperta* no less important in the Renaissance than its New World, new stars, new heavens and earth, its printing, gunpowder, and mariner's compass. For Montaigne and most of his readers, his *Essais*, tentatives, experiments into new matter seemed a new form. He apparently thought so himself, for when he tried to explain what he was up to, he turned to an established genre in another art:

> Considering the proceeding of a Painters worke I have; a desire hath possessed mee to imitate him: he maketh choice of the most convenient place and middle of everie wall, there to place a picture, laboured with all his skill and sufficiencie; and all void place about it he filleth up with antike Boscage or Crotesko work; which are fantasticall pictures, having no grace, but in the variety and strangenesse of them. And what are these my compositions in truth, other than antike workes, and monstrous bodies, patched and hudled up together of divers members, without any certaine or well ordered figure, having neither order, dependencie, or proportion, but casuall, and framed by chance?
>
> ("Of Friendship")

By the time he came to comment on the essay-form, Francis Bacon noted in his nominalist way that, although the ancients had no *name* for it, they nonetheless had the *thing*, in the epistles of Seneca, from which he and Montaigne so often drew. The essay is an interesting generic case in point, for although it was immediately imitated (among others by Etienne Pasquier), and although men wrote in this form privately and for money throughout the seventeenth century, only in the eighteenth century did it become an officially noticed genre, praised by Addison, condemned by Johnson. Perhaps one of its most radical expansions was a reason for its eventual recognition—Locke's *Essay concerning humane Understanding*, a book about empiricism empirically written, an attempt, an assaying, an essay, to redefine the ways human beings think. Like Montaigne's and Bacon's essays, Locke's book was altered and enlarged with every edition; once he began on that enterprise, he continued it all his life. No one could say, I think, that Locke's closely-argued first book resembles the essays of either Montaigne or Bacon; but in the later books of his *Essay*, particularly in the disjunctive fourth book, we can recognize from the chapter-titles the kind from which the whole enterprise sprang. "Of the Association of Ideas," "Of Relation," "Of Enthusiasm," "Of Power," "Of Knowledge in General" can all be read singly, as studies of particular subjects, as well as in their linked order with essays before and after. It seems appropriate that in this particular new literary genre, its title stressing its modest experimentalism, the *nova reperta* of a very new philosophy should be expressed.

If I had more time, I would try a very simple enterprise— namely, an examination of the *forms* various new-style thinkers chose to present their ideas in. Briefly, we remember that both Bacon and Campanella used the utopia, a new form, for their new concepts of social organization; that Kepler and Christiaen Huygens wrote cosmic voyages owing much to recent voyage-literature and to Lucian; that Galileo chose to present his revolutionary works on celestial and terrestrial mechanics in the hallowed humanist form of dialogue—that he dared, then, defend Copernicanism in this semidiscursive form; that Bruno relied heavily on the debate-form, as well as on poetic forms. It may seem surprising that anyone should choose to write of an infinite universe in hexameters, but Bruno did just that: and Henry More, his admirer, chose the English pentameter to present his Christianized Lucretian poem, *Democritus Platonissans*. Actually, however much Empedocles and Lucretius had suffered under Aristotelian canons of criticism, they got their own back in Giovanni Pontano's, Maurice Scève's, Gui Le Fèvre de la Boderie's, Pontus de Tyard's, and even Edmund Spenser's philosophical poems. Lyric poetry certainly made the most of that "bit of philosophy" Ronsard permitted it: the Platonism of sonneteers was not always restricted to love, as we know; and the emblem at its purest was a veiled idea worthy of any Renaissance esotericist.

But I haven't world enough, nor time, to exploit this multitudinous notion of Renaissance kind, and so must be brief about too much, about antiquity, about imagination, about those *nova reperta*, the New World, the new heavens. For it is to these I now turn—those discoveries made by the dwarfs upon giants' shoulders, discoveries unknown to the ancient giants. We all know printing, gunpowder, and the mariner's compass, the official triad; quinine, the mechanical clock, the stirrup, Don Quixote's windmills and other such things join the sacred three in Johannes Stradanus' pictures for Cosimo de Medici's Studiolo and in Guido Pancirolli's encyclopedic work (cited by Burton, of course), both called *Nova Reperta*, the new Findings, the new Inventions. Of course to organize things this way returns us to an older trope, *de inventoribus*, the celebration of the gods and men who found or invented this or that—Cadmus the alphabet, Hermes literature [and, of course, interpretations with it], Ceres bread, Bacchus wine, etc. In generic histories we have found this pattern—Aristotle on tragedy, Cicero on oratory. Polydore Vergil's book *De Inventoribus* was the Renaissance *locus classicus* for this material, as we know from Don Quixote's humanist, who tells us of Polydore Vergil's lapses:

> He forgot to tell us who was the first man in the world to have catarrh, and the first to use ointments to cure himself of the French pox; but all these points I set out with the utmost precision on the testimony of twenty-five authorities.

Sancho provides more *inventores*—Adam, the first man to scratch his head; the first tumbler, Lucifer; and Don Quixote accidentally finds another inventor, of playing cards, to delight his humanist friend.

I am trying to work in that tradition too, when I consider writers striving for new forms to express new ideas. In some sense Bacon's *New Aphorisms for Old*, La Rochefoucauld's redefinitions of human motivation in maxim-form and Pascal's unstinting analysis of the human capacity for alienation are efforts to substitute new formulations, brief and memorable, for what Bacon elsewhere called the wisdom of the ancients, so easily packageable into mnemonic forms. Not that they were altogether "new"—but though we can see something of Marcus Aurelius' deliberately broken techniques of insight in Pascal's *Pensées*, even in translation we could never mistake the one for the other. In a way, the concept of "self" was a *novum repertum*, as was its Gargantuan child, the epistemological revolution in seventeenth-century philosophy; in literary forms, we can find the bases for the exploration before the theory was provided by Descartes, Arnoldus Geulinx, Spinoza, Pierre Nicole, and Locke.

Montaigne's *Essais* offer a major example, of course; we may not be surprised that his "Apologie" and "De l'Expérience" are still read "historically" in courses in the history of philosophy. The reappearance of autobiography is another indicator: from Cardano to Edward Herbert this form has associations with men interested in the new philosophies, but even women and children took sufficient interest in their own lives to record them—witness Glueckl van Hameln and Brilliana Harley, as well as little Giles Isham, dutifully keeping his introspective diary. From Benvenuto Cellini to John Bunyan is a long step, but we can see in Bunyan's *Grace Abounding* a remarkable increase in self-analysis over the earlier work; Giles Isham presents a touching picture of a young boy trying to assess himself, a task slightly beyond him. In John Evelyn's endless redactions of his diary, we find a man as fully aware as Cellini of his need to project himself as a personality on his world. Glueckl's and Brilliana Harley's works are hardly literary documents, but Cardano exploited the meditation and the essay, Herbert of Cherbury the drama and romance, and Bunyan understood the intention if not the text of Augustine's *Confessions*. Secular and spiritual, the phenomenon itself points to a radical change in attitude, in which penmanship may be accounted one factor in increasing self-consciousness.

Perhaps even more interesting than biography in this context is the memoir, in which as a rule the author presented a highly stylized version of "himself" in one temporal segment of his experience. That segment and that version of self were within his own control: like the dramatist, he could choose the most suitable time-slice and discard all else about his life. We may well suspect La Rochefoucauld and Cardinal de Retz (whose memoirs seem to have required each other) of patterning themselves and their Fronde on the heroes and plots of tragedies of honor, though we need not assume that Corneille was the only supplier of that pattern. Intrigue in the wider world seems essential to their view of self-study—as important for La Rochefoucauld's view of La Rochefoucauld, Retz' of Retz, as for Mme. de Lafayette's fictions of *conscience*. From so closely connected a view of highly mannered life and a highly mannered literary mode, we might expect Saint-Simon's study of his years at Louis XIV's court to emerge; there, personality is inseparable from a shifting but complexly organized society, its rules understood by its participants and by its participant-observer—a society Copernican in its organization around the Sun King but Ptolemaic in the inexorable limitations of its universe. Saint-Simon himself is nearly transparent: unlike Retz and La Rochefoucauld, their own heroes, his personality emerges (like Burton's, perhaps?) rather as a style of vision than in the slightest breach of *politesse* occasioned by literary self-absorption. Hidden here is another rich fictional vein, as André Malraux has recognized in his *Antimemoires*; *recherches* into these *temps perdus* surely yielded much to Proust, as to Marcel's grandmother.

Another *novum repertum* is the picaresque novel, so brilliantly discussed by Claudio Guillen; here a man (—and, ultimately, a woman) outside the social structure lives through his experiences, seen always in relation to social class and occupation. Representatives of the various classes are given us through the picaro's eyes, and are usually stereotyped characters in a Theophrastan pattern. The countergenre offers its creative dialectic; in pastoral romance, a sensitive hero or heroine withdraws from the wicked social world to meditate, contemplate, love, write poetry, develop his or her inner potentialities. In the picaresque the insensitive central character—a kind of *tabula rasa* at the story's start, like Locke's hypothetical newborn baby—becomes more protectively and wisely insensitive as his experiences teach him the iniquities of the world from which he is forever alien, until he learns to accommodate himself to that world not so much bettered as ironized by experience. The whole mode mocks the *delicatesses* of pastoral, lyric whatever its formal genre. Indeed, as large pastoral forms developed in the Renaissance, they too tended to incorporate much mixture—not just the dialogues and competitions of classical bucolic, but also tales-within-tales, myths, magic, and so on. A play like *Cymbeline* or *The Winter's Tale*, late in the development of pastoral drama, welcomes many other modes and genres: I came across not long ago a Latin pastoral play called *Rubenus*, the subtitle of which was *Hilarotragoedia satyropastoralis*, full of singing, dancing, and even choruses of imitated birdsong. This play seemed a signature to the Guarini-quarrel, in a way: in it, everything has been firmly interlocked into one total dramatic mode. Lyric wins, though; the pipe sounds through and over the other generic instruments, and even the birdcalls insist on the pastoral as metaphor.

The picaresque unquestionably mixes many literary categories, too, but in another style—the low style of coney-catching pamphlets, farce and fabliaux incidents, folktale motifs. Lazarillo de Tormes, *ur*-picaro to some, was born on a river—as was I, as a matter of fact, born to my poor mother, late to the hospital. But I was born into a family and a social class even so: my father was present, and we were in a car on the ferry. Not so Lazarillo, whose father had vanished and whose mother had no fixed abode, to say nothing of cart. For the hero's peripateticism we can find models in Greek romance, but as critics of the genre emphasize, the peculiarities of the picaresque, with its lowlife ironies and its committed outsiderisms, preclude the conciliations which romance-solutions offer intolerable troubles.

For as the memoirist does, the picaresque author perceives society as an immutable construct. One cannot say that the typical picaro develops—even in those picaresques crossed with the spiritual autobiography or the dramatic *auto* in which conversion is necessary; one can only say that his sense

of reality deepens with his serial experiences. His consciousness, if not his literary personality, fills out and takes substance—and with an ironical privacy peculiar to this genre,
for, though readers are aware that the picaro is aware of his
accomplished consciousness, only that awareness is communicated, never a definition of any specific increase in consciousness. In this kind, we are offered a model of how experiences
can be translated into experience. The picaro is his own problem, and he solves it—we may know that he is critical of his
solution, but he does not let us in on his program of criticism.

Perhaps you can tell that I am pussyfooting around one of
the biggest problems in Renaissance scholarship, its historiography. There, too, in a genre removed from poetics, society is
seen as a problem, but in so many different ways that it would
take a real master of arts to tackle the dimensions of Renaissance history-writing. Classical models were imitated, of
course—Pieter Cornelisz. Hooft translated and imitated Tacitus because that paradigm of history and historical writing
was a successful one in the period; Attic-style theorists de-
pended on Tacitus to teach them how to bend style to "what
happened." Generally, in humanist histories—of cities, families, spans of time—epideictic rhetoric tended to pull away
from events in their disorderly complexity. Christian historiography took for granted another sort of orderliness, as events
were seen duly to work themselves out in providential patterns.
One reason it is so hard to write at large about Renaissance
historiography is that there were so many competing and
overlapping notions of what "history" was or ought to be—but,
at the same time, from this muddle emerged meaningful experiments in establishing ways of recording and commenting
on societies changing over time. I want to touch, all too briefly,
on various histories which break patterns and, even if they do
not finally establish new ones, strive toward that end.

The first of these is a book generally neglected by real historians, and understandably so, since it runs an extremely eclectic course from the world's beginning (Genesis) to the foundations of Rome as an imperial power. This is Sir Walter Ralegh's *History of the World*, of which only the first third is finished (the author, as he said, having "hewn out the rest," was not spared to finish the whole). It is partly a providential history, particularly as it treats of Jewish history; partly a critical historiographical study, the author weighing his sources against one another; partly an anthropological comparative work; partly a book of essays in the form of digressions. These digressions—on man as microcosm; on the intellectual capacity of men; on the three types of government; on the law of nature, etc.—often seriously subvert the providential pattern of history proclaimed in the Preface and dominating, in the form of a large eye, the iconography of Ralegh's beautiful engraved titlepage.

Ralegh's is an "universal" history—not for nothing was Diodorus Siculus one of his sources—with narrative, fiction, digression the rule of that work; this history is universal not in its temporal scope alone, but also in its by-now familiar combination of different forms of discourse, to convey something of the range and variety of human experience. Like Burton's book, like Athenaeus', Ralegh's book takes one major topic as an excuse to treat all topics, this time human history. Certainly it is in our sense partly a "history," that is a comparative study of cultures changing over time; but it is also, and probably more so, a history in the Plinian sense of description and commentary on everything in the world of man and nature and in the intellectual world as well—an anthology in the humanist kind.

Etienne Pasquier, Montaigne's curious friend, essayed quite a different sort of history; although some of the generalizations I just made about Ralegh's book might apply to Pasquier's *Recherches*, they spring from a different set of specifics. Not content with chronicling local antiquity, which he knew very well, nor yet with laudatory history of the kind Bacon began of England, Pasquier studied documents and texts, which he inserted into his chronological narrative of France. Now this is so much a part of modern practice that we may not realize quite what difficulties of composition it posed for historians then. If we think of literary archaism for a moment—Rabelais' use of old forms; Spenser's rustic style in the *Calendar*; the play within the play in *Hamlet*—we can understand something of the peculiar force of archaism within another language-matrix. Pasquier by no means solved the problem of decorum, but he at least recognized it, as a writer and as an historian. As an historian, the documents guided him—where they lacked, he did not fill in "what happened" by imaginative reconstruction; consequently his *Recherches* are very spotty. Indeed, one way of looking at his work is that he was not so much composing as assembling a collection of sources on which he wrote essays in commentary and explication. He adapted current philological techniques to his own needs in a series of essays on institutions and institutional titles (dame, damoiselle, vidame; sieur, seigneur; couvre-feu ou carfou); he noted Huizingesque habits—games (tennis and chess), proverbs, idioms (e.g., castles in Spain); he indicated when the Gypsies first came into France. He commented on the *nova reperta*, too, noting that the Chinese originated printing, and citing a fifteenth-century poet to deny that the mariner's compass was a modern invention.

His medieval researches led him to consider literature as an institution; he is one of the few French critics to recognize a cultural continuity across periods in his remarks on Provençal and modern literature, organized on generic and *de inventoribus* lines. This spotty, dotty history is *quand même* an effort truly cultural, objective in a sense very rare in the Renaissance, a worthy forerunner of La Curne de la Palaye and the antiquarian cultural historians of the eighteenth century, a proper topic for *Past and Present* now.

It is Pasquier's reliance on documents that I have stressed. Actually, institutional histories regularly dealt critically with documents relating to their subjects. The ones I know best are, it is true, polemical—Paolo Sarpi's history of the Council of Trent, Giacomo Bosio's account of the Maltese Knights written after the collapse of Valletta, Caspar Brandt's history of the Arminians. Polemical as they are, these works are not rhetorical *plaidoyers*, nor do their documents dictate intellectual positions: what emerges from these works, however committed to their various subjects, is the sense of history as problematic, historiography as a critical enterprise. That is to say, mixed in tone as the writing-surface of these works may be, none is the compendious encyclopedia of Ralegh's *History*: societies and institutions move into the foreground, their details worked into relief, their records treated with respect and with critical attention. Historiography becomes primarily a critical enterprise.

So preeminently for Clarendon in his *History of the Rebellion*, which might have been a memoir, since the author played a part in the events he describes—and, indeed, the author did compose a history of his own life toward the end of it, when his public service was over. But Clarendon consistently excludes himself from his book as an actor in its events: "Mr. Hyde," or "a friend" does what he actually did, and he intrudes as author very little save for the summings up—on King Charles' reign, for instance, or on Cromwell's character. Though for some observers Thucydides has seemed Clarendon's nearest model, that model is far from sufficient—save for the two historians' conviction that their upheavals were of extraordinary significance and for their determined efforts to describe the character, if not the *areté*, of the participants in those upheavals. There are, certainly, impressive personal descriptions—of Strafford, of Hamden, of Fairfax—with something of the judiciousness but none of the malice of Retz' and La Rochefoucauld's characters of their friends and acquaintances; there are passages, such as the trial of the king, which owe to dramatic and narrative models. But Clarendon's chief gifts are, I think, the historian's determination to present *Gestalt*, situation, and to account for events by their antecedents. He understood the significance of what we now know to be sociology, and treated of cause and effect in a primarily social way—a way, for instance, not very different from that of social novelists a hundred years later. I may overpraise Clarendon's talents as an historian, but I think I do not overpraise his book, which is a remarkably composed whole. First of all, he never cites a mass of classical and other writers as authority; his references, when they occur, are to documents and personal communications directly relevant to his subject. Nor does he digress, really. The interruptions to the flow of his narrative serve the problems raised by that narrative: they describe the personalities of major figures in an event, they explain the nature of a particular institution or custom, they motivate some apparently incomprehensible aspect of the political situation. The subject is treated single-mindedly and as a whole: the narrative owes its variety to the appropriate disposition of kinds, as one genre balances and complements another in a book which, defining an historical subject in a strikingly new way, controls the subject by devices and structures from the familiar generic repertory.

In a final example, I want to contrast Agrippa d'Aubigné's historical work with the historical parts of his tragic epic poem about Protestant sufferings in the Religious Wars. D'Aubigné wrote an historical account, very different in form from Foxe's *Book of Martyrs* if not so different in motivation and tone, which he called *Histoire Universelle*. The title is, of course, a significant misnomer for a narrative beginning with the birth of Henry of Navarre and ending with his assassination as King of France; in another sense, though, as providential history, the segment treated in this book may be seen as "universal." Certainly the book is full of pathos, if not of tragedy: one feels in so passionate a story of persecution both the pity and the fear tragedy dictates. The chief characters on the Roman Catholic side are presented in detail, their schemes and brutalities laid bare, as if the author saw with God's omnipotent eye. Again and again the fidelity of the Reformed martyrs is exemplified, from the flashback parallels in Albigensian history to the sufferings under the Ligue. As from the tragic machine, the voice of God speaks through this history—but beside these experiments in literary high style, we also have in D'Aubigné's account one of the most careful studies of the social geography of war in any book of the whole period.

The presence of so many dramatic elements in the *Histoire universelle* is not so surprising when we consider what D'Aubigné did with the same materials in his heroic poem, *Les Tragiques,* an epic or near-epic owing a good deal to Lucan's *Pharsalia*—historical poetry conceived in epic terms. *Les Tragiques* remarkably combines, however, Renaissance concepts of tragedy with a generally epic story in which God and Satan struggle for mastery of the world. Pity and fear are certainly present, peculiarly divided between the two antagonistic groups of humans. We must fear for the Protestants, martyred so piteously and endlessly by their implacable opponents; but in the last two of the poem's seven books, "Vengeances" and "Jugement," we find that Providence does not spare the wicked, to whom in turn pity and fear must be granted. Since the Protestant hero, Coligny, is assumed into heaven like Petrarca's and Macrobius' Scipio, why isn't this book, as one critic asked, called *Les Comiques*?

Of course it isn't very funny, even if the heavenly ending is a "happy" one, but the real answer lies in the structure of the poem, organized along the lines of dramatic tragedy, with a prologue setting the scene (*les Misères*) and various acts laid out—*Princes, La Chambre Dorée, Les Feux, Les Fers*—and a climactic action, and act, in *Vengeances*. In the epilogue, *Jugement*, things are tidied up as morality and the Deity decide. By telescoping Scriptural with modern history in typological fusions, D'Aubigné manages to make a single historical situation symbolically universal, "universelle." By involving humanity in its own tragedy, exemplified here by the warring sons of France, D'Aubigné orders his epic under the banner of Melpomene, the tragic muse, whom he invokes at the poem's beginning.

In fusing history with poetry, as well as fusing kinds of poetry, D'Aubigné has reasserted not just the truth of both, but their interdependence in events. In his unorthodox epic, he too exploited the concept of the epic's multiple form. But, really, it is Homer's substance rather than his epic construction which has its echoes here—a real battle between real heroes, certainly, but no twenty-four books, no ring-construction; rather, the organizing devices are drawn from another genre. D'Aubigné tried to make his *Histoire* "universelle" by recapitulating into its short time-span not just French spiritual history but the history of persecuted Israel and of the Christian martyrs as well. So his poem is, really, "universel" also, uniting in one work concepts of history, epic, and tragedy. If for nothing else, D'Aubigné is interesting in his conceptualizing of history into patterns offered by literary kinds.

Once more we are presented with a deliberately eccentric, avowedly inclusive book, in which a writer has dared to incorporate his own vision into a world seen as total—and to do so by the means offered by his writer's craft. The forms of epic and of tragedy are perceived in history—in epic battles, in tragic denouements, in hymns which work to elevate mere "event" into "story." For D'Aubigné, anyway, good Protestant that he was, the factualness of his account also elevated poetry: that is, at the same time that generic metaphors and structures organize reality, that reality substantiates poetry. "Ein Burgerkrieg, ein epos"—Roda-Roda's categories might be adapted to this situation. The principle of *mimesis* by which Aristotle rejected history from the poetic canon is turned inside out, as actual historical events significantly rearrange themselves into a work of art, and by so doing validate it as "true."

IV
Kindness and
Literary Imagination

I want to look now at certain mixes, migrations, and alterations in generic category, to see, if I can, what the *literary* gain may be, both in having genres and in refusing to allow generic categories to dictate or predestine the size, scope, content, and manner in any particular literary work. Let me start with a small form, the sonnet: earlier, I tried to show how in some important instances, the sonnet-world and the epigram-world had been, by an errant Newtonian magnetism, drawn together, the epigram in some sense "raised" by its associations with the sonnet, the sonnet's insistent sweetness radically counterpointed by the epigram's salt and vinegar. Association with the epigram may have satisfied a *nostalgie de la boue* on the part of the usually airy sonnet, some secret instinct for slumming, which we can identify also in Cecco Angiolieri's dialect sonnets, or in Francesco Berni's and Giovanni Burchiello's nonsense-sonnets.

But there is an impressive record of the sonnet's "aspirations": indeed, one might say that this little form had always aspired to be what it was not, to keep up with the Joneses of more spacious forms. Very early, it was the sonnet which by simple accretion turned into a semi-stanzaic sequence, a narrative of love. Dante's *Vita Nuova* is highly experimental in its combination of lyric forms (sonnet, madrigal, canzone) with prose commentary of several sorts. Beside this tremendous effort, we can the more clearly read Petrarca's determination to regularize his carefully constructed poetic sequence, which dispensed with the prose by absorbing into poetry much of what Dante had relegated to prose interspersions. For Dante's prose had been the medium of his peculiar *explications de texts*—that last genre, overdeveloped in our time, was in its infancy, perhaps *in utero*, when Dante tried his hand at it; and his prose was as well as his means of skipping over incidents, time-spans, and other narrative matters not conveniently worked into the verses. Although Petrarca wrote his sequence entirely in poetry, he by no means sacrificed the self-critical and literary-critical elements Dante had treated in prose, but rather wrote it all in, commenting on his work in the course of writing it. With Petrarca, I suppose, a new invention was offered as model to subsequent sonneteers: one could write in single sonnets, each a lyric unit, or in a sequence or cycle, which offered a more or less connected narrative of love, with elements of psychological investigation and literary criticism intrinsically related, in the genre, to the love-situation. Wordsworth was honoring a very old custom when he wrote his sonnets on the sonnet. We know the success of the form—there are too many sequences, really, for anyone to master them all. The interesting thing about them, however, is their variation: Du Bellay's *Regrets* is very little concerned with love; Sidney's *Astrophil and Stella* is arranged with its songs in the middle, breaking into the sequence of sonnets in significant ways; Ronsard comments on his earlier sonneteering in his later sequences, and on his earlier loves as well; contrast of kinds is one element in the power of Shakespeare's series.

Though it is true that sonnet-sequences "grew"—Du Bellay's *Olive* from 50 to 115 sonnets between its first and second appearances—it is not just the length of this kind which I take as proof of the sonnet's aspiring to more than fourteen lines can conveniently hold. The "more" of the sonnet-sequence lies not only in its shadowy psychological plot, but also in the deepening of analytical themes already present in the thematics of the single sonnet—the sonneteer's self-examination, expressive of internal condition, his commentary on his own progress in both poetry and love. The "plot" of Dante's and Petrarca's sequences, moreover, was one of psychological and spiritual elevation; the poet himself learnt, through his love of a lady, to love her abstractly, then to love heaven and truth. Not for nothing is the Queen of Heaven invoked in the last poem of the *Canzoniere.*

With such a pattern established, small wonder that Renaissance Platonism easily domesticated itself in sonnet-sequences, infusing new ideological strength into the love-theories subscribed to already by sonneteers. This Platonism emerged overtly in Lorenzo de' Medici's work, and the sonnets and longer poems of Pontus de Tyard—indeed, Pontus dispensed with the orthodox real or fictional lady to write simply about truth and love of truth. As early as 1555, Jacques Peletier du Mans could say that the sonnet was "quasi tout philosophique en conceptions"—an ambiguous phrase requiring a good deal of data to explicate properly. Many sonneteers lived up to that charge: Drayton called his lady "Idea," Davies of Hereford composed sonnets on "th' Abstract Nature," and Chapman dedicated sonnets "To his Mistresse Philosophie." Necessarily in such poems, figures of though were very important, pushing into second place the figures of speech so important in the Petrarchan tradition. Merely by its concentration on a particular subject-matter, the sonnet became a ground for the celebrated "intellectual" or metaphysical style of the early seventeenth century.

Dante and Petrarca of course made overt the connection between loving a lady and loving celestial things—a short step, though one long in being taken, to the subgenre of the spiritual sonnet. Certainly the implications of such a type were developed by Bembo, and Girolamo Malipiero "translated" a *Petrarca spirituale* which cleaned up his original. Benedetto Varchi, Piccolomini, and Minturno (who was very proud of his eighty-one sonnets on God) all wrote *Sonetti spirituali*, and we can find other sixteenth-century poets—the Abbé de Billy, Anne des Marquets, Fernando Herrera, Luis de Leon, Henry Lok, Henry Constable, William Alabaster—forerunners of the better-known sacred sonneteers Jean de Sponde, John Donne, Lope de Vega, Gongora, Huygens, Andreas Gryphius, Paul Flemming. From a comparative study of this literary kind, I think a good deal might be learnt about the constant impulsive pressure of a style upon its next generation, as well as about differences (or lack of them) in religious utterance by Roman Catholic and Protestant poets. I suspect too, that something of the intricacy of what is called "metaphysical" style may in this case owe more to the *topoi* of religious problems and paradoxes than to concentration upon stylistic novelty for its own sake.

There are sonnets to be found in many different modes: Varchi's and Richard Barnefield's in the pastoral, Luigi Alamanni's *Coltivazione* in the georgic, Du Bellay's *Antiquitez de Rome* and *Regrets* fusing sonnet and epigram, Jean de la Taille's *Sonnets satyriques*—to say nothing of the heroic sonnets, so close to odes in manner, of Bembo, the elder Tasso, Della Casa, Jean Godard, Jean de la Taille, and Milton. Vauquelin de la Fresnaye makes overt the association of sonnet and ode—"Si tu fais un Sonnet ou si tu fais un Ode, / Il faut qu'un mesme fil au sujet s'accommode," he wrote, enjoining for both the requirement of elevated style:

On peut le Sonnet dire une chanson [canzone] petite;
Fors qu'en quatorze vers toujours on le limite:

Et l'Ode et la Chanson peuvent tout librement
Courir par le chemin d'un bel entendement.

In the *Hécatombe de Diane*, Agrippa d'Aubigné utilized
themes from the heroic epitaph, exploiting as well the meanings gathered around Petrarca's sonnets to Laura *in morte*; in
the sonnet-*proposte* and *riposte* of so many different cinque-
cento academicians and of the Pléiade members too, we can
perceive the sonnet functioning as *manners*, as a social form
like the many courtesy-exchanges outlined in Castiglione's
Courtier.

Quite simply, this form, the sonnet, so firmly established
in its size and metrical structure, proved extraordinarily open
to the topics, styles, and tones of other literary modes and
genres, even to literary criticism: Shakespeare, by providing
a plot-element in the rival poet, justified literary criticism
and theory as a sonnet-topic and wonderfully enlivened the
critical tendency we have seen built into sonneteering. More
than this, sonnets occurred at socially proper moments in
larger forms—we know, for instance, that in *As You Like It*
Orlando fastened sonnets to trees (presumably sonnets in
the pastoral mode); there are also love-sonnets in Sidney's
Arcadia. *Romeo and Juliet* is famous for its use of sonnets in
the dialogue, even stichomythic sonnets; and sonnet-language
provides much of the elevation of what is, in that play, an
adaptation to the tragic mode of comic structure, characters,
and events. Less noticed, but I think even more important, is
the use of sonnet-language at crucial points in *Othello*, to say
nothing of the expansion into tragic action of the psychological "plot" of a sequence of love-sonnets. As a form, then, the
sonnet was hospitable to the attitudes and subjects of literary
kinds normally quite removed from it. As a thematic genre
itself, as a *topos* even, the sonnet could be used in conjunction with other forms. To say this quite another way, the son-

net can be seen to act mythically—as a way of life, or perceiving the world: as a system of values in *Othello*; as a gesture, metaphorically, in *As You Like It*.

In Bruno's dialogue, *De gli eroici furori, Of Heroic Frenzies*, the love-sonnet is the point of departure. In the dedication to Sir Philip Sidney and in the dialogue's first book, the love-discussion is carried on in terms of real and definite sonnets, some of them by Luigi Tansillo (one interlocutor in the dialogue), more by Bruno himself. Insofar as it explicates and interprets these sonnets, Bruno's dialogue can be taken, in one of its many aspects, as an expanded critical self-commentary on sonnets, a form familiar since Dante and manifested in Lorenzo's *Commento*—though to say this is to shift stress away from the principal point of *Gli eroici furori*. In a traditional conflation of *eros* with *heros* (love with heroism) reaching back to Plato, Bruno insisted on the heroic character, not of sonnets simply, but of love itself. His conception of heroism is not in the public tradition, though celebrated in odes or ode-like heroic sonnets, but is private, personal, mental—quite as love is conceived by most sonneteers. Bruno's view is of a love philosophized—hence his *Eroici furori* also belongs with the many Renaissance programmatic *dialoghi d'amore* descending from the *Symposium*. After explicating philosophically the images of sonnets, the dialogues' interlocutors turn to emblems; here Bruno's esoteric conception of a truth hidden from all but the sharp-eyed seeker emerges even more plainly than before. The emblems themselves are taken generically: with their derivations from collections by Paolo Giovio, Alciato, and Beza, the emblems become metaphors for the heroic, the moral, and the religious realms. Bruno organized their thematics within the hierarchy of his own values. At the same time, though, he showed the relation of the emblem-image to the sonnet-image as symbolic of a truth far larger than their compressions might seem to allow—the confidence in the significant compression, so apparent in Erasmus' *Adagia,* of a truth the more momentous for the laconism of its form. So the rich, hyperbolical imagery of sonnet-lovers, established over centuries of self-conscious practice in a form, can be absorbed into the emblem-tradition of esotericism: this too may have something to do with the apparently mysterious development of *concettismo* in lyric poetry.

Bruno notoriously jeered at the conventional language of sonneteers—at those shrieks deafening the stars, those laments reverberating in the caves of hell, those sighs to make the gods swoon with pity, all for "those eyes, those cheeks, those teeth, those lips, that hair, that glove, that shoe, that window . . . that stink, that tomb, that carrion" that is a woman; but his jeering at the object of love did not affect his making use of the *words* customarily used to express that love. As Erasmus had advised students to fit adages to their own needs and ideas, Bruno adapted the phrases of sonnet-language, even whole sonnets and emblems, to his own needs. Which is to say, he used them in service of a philosophy heightened over its forerunners, a Platonism more abstract than Plato's and more comprehensive even than Plotinus', a Platonism insisting on the importance and reality of the physical universe and on the emotional life of the little universe, man, as well as on the immense—that is, unmeasurable—universe organized by the proportions of infinity.

De gli eroici furori begins in very precise criticism and interpretation of poetry and poetic theory: "I know," Cicada says, "framers of poetic rules who find it difficult to accept Homer as a poet and who reject Vergil, Ovid, Martial, Hesiod, Lucretius, and many other writers in verse, after having subjected them to examination according to rules of Aristotle's *Poetics.*" But poetry is simply one way into metaphysics and ontology, and a natural way, since poetry itself is taken as the expression of esoteric meaning. In so doing, Bruno reversed the usual process, attributed to Homer by the Aristotelians, of putting philosophy to poetic uses: he put poetry to philosophical uses, deployed the kinds in the service of that discipline Aristotle had removed from poetry's domain. But it is an Horatian trick, really, to teach by delighting.

Bruno's literary craftsmanship is at least as interesting as his hermeticism, and a good deal easier to check. The dialogues are deft with literary concepts, *topoi*, and the kinds; obviously, he was an accomplished writer, with, in the dialogues at least, a taste for parody and satire. Earlier, I spoke of Bruno's use of poetic forms (evidently on the model of Lucretius, whom he often paraphrased) to present his highly abstracted conceptions: his *De Immenso et Innumerabile*—not surprisingly, perhaps, his longest poem—offers a full exposition of philosophical views, along with critiques of alternative systems and notions. His book on geometric proportion, *De mensura*, is in verse, as is his published *De triplici minimo*; several other works existing in fragments were obviously designed as poetry. In one of his memory works, *On the Composition of Images, Signs, and Ideas* (1591), he offered some of these symbolic images in verse-form, in what Puttenham calls "icons," or allegorical figures—of Care, Fear, Doubt, Sorrow, and the like. Bruno's *Candelaio* is a comedy, well-made so far as I can tell, perhaps too well-made by half. Bruno's dialogues, almost as a tic, begin with literary matters. In *De la causa*, Bruno ran through the poetic preoccupations of his time: the *genera dicendi*, ancient authority, *la questione della lingua* and spelling, collections of different sorts lexical and rhetorical ("un spicilegio, un dizionario, un Calepino, un lessico, un cornucopia, un Nizzolio"—compendia of available knowledge and techniques). The interlocutors in this dialogue play games with the gender (genre) of nouns—*corpo* (body) is masculine and bad, *anima* (soul) feminine and good; chaos masculine, order (dispozisione) feminine; error masculine, truth feminine, etc. One of the interlocutors—*Polinnio,* masculine, bad form of the good Polyhymnia—is a pedant worthy of academic comedy or the *commedia erudita,* who meets every new or surprising philosophical proposition with an adage from the Bible or antiquity: his own speeches make almost no sense, so thick are the tags of his Latinity. All these games with literature, mind you, are in the service of Teofilo's final discussion in the last book on the logic of the infinite universe.

For Sidney as for Aristotle and Horace, poetry was great for its capacity to teach on the sly, by means of delight. Bruno delights by establishing literary *topoi* as steps to his teaching: that is, he abstracted literature, as he does so many elements of his thought, into its signs and symbolic values. The kinds were useful because they were so readily made into metaphors. In the first dialogue of the *Eroici furori,* Tansillo explains, with some adjustment to his own bias, the functions of the kinds in terms of appropriate plants—myrtle for poets of love, laurel for heroic poets who "instruct the soul through speculative and moral philosophy":

I say there are and can be as many sorts of poets as there are kinds of feeling and of human invention, all of whom may wear garlands not only of all kinds and types of plants, but of all kinds and types of matter. For the crowns of poets are not made only of myrtle and laurel, but also of vineleaves for fescennine verses, ivy for bacchanals, olive for sacrifices and laws, poplar, elm, and wheat for agriculture, cypress for funerals, and innumerable other kinds of leaves for other occasions. It is even true, as one gallant said,

> Brother Porro, poet of flounders,
> You at Milan crown yourself with a garland
> Of puddings, tripe, and sausage.

Understanding the symbolic language of literary function, Cicada, the inquirer after truth in the dialogue, then realizes that the poet whose text is their key to universal truth—Bruno Nolano—is entitled to wear a crown of the diverse branches symbolizing his topics. In Marvell's "The Garden," the speaker wryly observes,

> How vainly men themselves amaze
> To seek the oak, the palm, the bayes,

when they might, like Bruno, wear Garlands to which "all Flow'rs and Trees" make contribution of their foliage: *Sylva*, mixed forest, mixed matter.

In Marvell's poem, as in Bruno's dialogue, the literary kinds are turned into metaphors—not reduced so much as compressed by this operation, like resonant adages and emblems, *implying* far more than they seem to hold. In Bruno's metaphors of foliage, he shows how the kinds, taken as a whole, can make up the furniture of a man's mind, can represent his whole culture. Castiglione's *Cortegiano* is, I suppose, as good an example as any of the way in which a civilized man's activities, physical and mental, single and social, are viewed as arts by which he, in cooperation with others and in imitation of a perfect idea, continuously civilizes himself. Its endless *paragoni*, clashes of wit, competitions of accomplishment—debates on sculpture and painting, ancient languages and the vernacular, politeness and rudeness, nature and art, love and love— turn out in the end to harmonize all the various role-aspects of a single personality into a perfect society. Castiglione's book is, among other things, an *Institutio*, a book of education, cast in dialogue-form—and, further, particular *formal* implications are developed precisely in the ordering of things into *paragoni*. Within the dialogue, though, we have many other mini-forms and kinds: exchanges of *facetiae*, *burle*, *novelle*, as well as many different partial *institutiones*—of military art, hunting, music, poetry, ruling, loving. That is, the humanist genres are composed into manageable form to serve the dominant generic mandate—and, at the same time to recapitulate a culture.

I think there is more to the work than this, though "this" is surely enough: behind the clear statements of a courtier's duty to himself as a man, and to the court of which he is an element and an ornament, the debate of art with nature is carried on. Urbino is a *locus amoenus*, established as such in the first paragraphs of the book—unthreatened by war, a place where men and women live in peace together in a total harmony. Save for a slightly snake-in-the-grass type, the mercantile citizen Pallavicino, who utters what grossness there is in the book, they cultivate themselves and respect the cultivation of others. A utopia, you may say, where "Fay ce que voudras" is what everyone wishes to do together. Yes, but the structure of ideas is also a pastoral one, in which the competition of nature and art is resolved, so that (as in pastoral) nature is perfected by art. Sir Satyrane needs the refinements of a true court as Sir Calidore needs the sustaining comforts of his sojourn in nature. In a sense, what Castiglione has done is to bring into the unmetaphored foreground a fundamental pastoral question about human nature and human attitude, and cast his discussion of it in various non-pastoral and even non-literary forms—but the dialectic remains, signaled by those topical signposts of a thematic genre.

Obviously, both Castiglione and Bruno are inclusionists— their ends are big, to re-form man, to re-form philosophy. Can we say, as Northrop Frye for instance has, that there is a genre designed to *include* others, a genre called "anatomy" or anthology? If such a genre were to be confidently established, then it ought to facilitate interpretation; but in this particular case, if there is such a genre, it does not orientate us as Hirsch, Gombrich, and by implication Frye, would have it do—the process of interpretation of *The Courtier* remains tricky. We still have to decide what kind is dominant in the book. Is it chiefly a dialogue? If I say it is, I throw myself in with Alexandrian librarians—which in fact sounds a nice companionship—who classify by formal means. Is it an *Institutio*, a blueprint for education? If this is what it is, then I must insist, like Roda-Roda, that subject governs genre: *Viele Frauen und viele Maenner, ein Unterweysung*. If I opt for dialogue, then what in this work develops dialogic generic implications? Is it the pull toward dramatic incident, the play of ideas, the philosophical or subphilosophical topic, the use of a dominant voice making sure the true message is clear? If I choose *Institutio*, then I must work through the various structures of that kind—is it organized as a *summa virtutum*, or by age, or according to the levels of ease by which accomplishments may be made? Certainly none of these categories seems to prevail entirely over the others, nor can I dispense with any. Though I would put up a fight for *The Courtier* as an urban-pastoral dialogue, I would also stress its purely poetic use of metaphor; as in its musical *institutio*, it establishes the *armonia* that is its theme. Different parts, then, can be worked by *sprezzatura* into one whole, each part essential to the harmony of courtier and of book. But this would not work, either, for the reader who was unaware that *armonia* was a social and moral value as well as the physical and psychological result of certain sounds: for him, that structural symbol would be meaningless.

I am saying, I think, that in this long period, the Renaissance, the literary theory that underlies all other is *not* really expressed in its rich and varied criticism: namely, that a literary kind stands for a kind of subject, a kind of content, literary and intellectual; and also that some references to a subject or content may be taken as metaphors for a whole kind. I am not now talking about a rigid system of genres—which, really, never existed in practice and barely even in theory—by which each subject defined separately commands its and only its assigned form. We have been looking at far too many examples of works that invoke mixed kind rather than a specific single kind to accept any such rule. I am talking rather about a body of almost unexpressed assumptions, many of them versions of classical theory or practice, which took for granted certain basic rules of expression. A language of kind, made up, like the Greek and Roman pantheons, of different categories of kind—a language full of idioms. But as in language, it is the idioms which we must learn in order not to be caught out.

If we had a rigid genre-system, then we would have even more forms with double names, like Guarini's tragicomedy. Shakespeare's sonnets taken as a whole would have to be called sonnegrams, or epigrets; Vasari's *Lives of the Artists* called *Saints' Lives of the Artists*—and if Professor Havelock is right, Thucydides' history called *Heroic History of the Pelepponese War*. These sound silly, but no sillier than tragicomedy must have sounded in Mercury's mouth when Plautus made it up, or comitragedy when the Jesuit theorists solemnly made *it* up, or *Hilarotragoedia satyropastoralis* was supposed to sound to its Bolognese audience. Someone must have laughed, though perhaps not Hamlet, when Shakespeare made Polonius speak, in a splendid self-reference to Shakespeare's own accomplishment, of plays "comical-tragical-historical-pastoral."

Rather, I am trying to express something of the *social* force and function of the kinds, as abbreviations for a "set" on the world, as definitions of manageable boundaries, some large, some small, in which material can be treated and considered. Social too in the sense that, these sets and boundaries understood, a great deal need *not* be said about them: one needn't recapitulate all pastoral values in a dialogue set in Urbino the well-named, when one can show by various signposts that pastoral values are understood as part of this work's urbanity. Since whatever generic definitions a writer or a culture espouses, examples willy-nilly accumulate in generic categories, the kinds can easily be seen as tiny subcultures with their own habits, habitats, and structures of ideas as well as their own forms. But as subcultures continually melt into or are absorbed by a neighboring culture, so did the kinds in our period melt into one another—often to enrich the possibilities of literature taken as system. We can put it technically, or professionally: there is an art to be mastered for the eclogue form (meter, topic, trope, etc.) and for the pastoral mode (in dramatic or lyric genres, in poetry or prose), as there is for tragedy and for the tragic mode (dramatic, epic, lyric; prose, poetry). Those arts mastered, there is no reason other than conviction why they should not be used together—but they cannot be used with utter indiscriminateness. We have to know *why* they are intermixed. That *Hilarotragoedia satyropastoralis* of which I keep speaking is an example of inadequate intermixture, really: on every page, we know that Bettini was writing an academic exercise, a vacation exercise—its kind is literary-critical, not dramatic. But when the mad Lear says "They cannot touch me for coining; I am the King himself . . . Nature's above art in that respect," the two modes, tragic and pastoral, converge to make us realize that commitment to the ethos of one of those modes is threatened at its roots by a demand for commitment to the other. Or, the audience must realize by that juxtaposition of generic references the poignancy of an old man's effort to find pastoral peace in a country where *otium* is not permitted.

Thinking about Shakespeare, we can readily see how for him genres could be treated as metaphors—I spoke of the uses of sonnets in *Romeo and Juliet*, but consider Puck as the parasite playwright in *A Midsummer Night's Dream*, a generic device literally in miniature. Shakespeare's usual attitude to genre is, I think, mythic, as in the two generic "parts" of *The Winter's Tale*, where the implications of tragedy and of pastoral are constantly alluded to, in the words spoken, in configurations of character, even in the gestures of the action. Surely when Marvell plays with the kinds as he does in "The Garden," we recognize the maker as *demiourgos* and craftsman, rather than as creator or *vates,* and can expect, reading Marvell, that an age of mock-forms from Dryden to Swift might indeed be possible. But it never seemed possible to me, reading Shakespeare, that a Dryden or a Tate would lay hands on his generic mythic mixtures to straighten them out again.

In *Don Quixote,* we are faced with a work which on the one hand reduces kinds—think of the inset stories in that work (*novelle, favole, parabole, istorie*), as well as all the other kinds worked into it, paradox and puppet-show, sermon and moral essay. On the other hand, this work mythicises the kinds: out of this antimythical creation, indeed, a new literary myth was made, as well as a new literary kind. We know a good deal about the genre to which Don Quixote wished to belong; we know, too, a great deal about chivalric romance-epic, ironic and tragic, from Ariosto and Tasso and from the critical quarrels over their poems. If literary criticism and theory need justification, then surely the fact of *Don Quixote* makes up for everything critics and theorists do wrong! For this book is, like so many of the uncanonical books discussed earlier, a book made out of books, a book in which literary myths of reality are faced up against that reality, to show the shallowness of rigid doctrines of *mimesis.* Again and again, fiction wins, even when reality seems to smash it, as when a *novum repertum,* the windmill, takes no notice of antique heroism. But lions lie down with Quixote the lamb, and when he is not allowed to be his own fiction any longer, he takes to his bed and dies.

In Don Quixote's literary dialogues, echoing, parodying, defending, undermining the critical theories of the Renaissance, we find the ground from which Cervantes built: more often than not, his hero wins literary arguments by sly applications of the very dogmas adduced against his generic perceptions of the world. Two literary systems face each other, that of fiction and that of critical precept; as any student of literature knows, in the competition of these two, fiction must win. A greater problem is raised by making a *paragone* of fiction with reality—but even though his old bones are bruised for it, Don Quixote turns out to have chosen the better part almost every time. In this comical-tragical-satirical epic, we are forced to examine, not only literary set or fix, but its relation to psychological set as well: the one is called art, the other madness, and both dictate fictions. And: reality is known by these fictions, as fiction by reality—the chivalric myth by its nonfit to the social and geographical routes Don Quixote chooses to travel, the social world by its failures to recognize what moral realities are embodied in Don Quixote's myth. The farce reveals the inner tragic play, the literalism the myth. Indeed, Don Quixote mocks his own aspirations, with Mambrino's helmet, with his destrier Rocinante, with his squire Sancho Panza—with a knight-errant who is himself. In incident after incident, the comic mode shades off into the tragic and precariously restores itself, with no visible interface between the two modes: we know them by each other, their interconnections as tight as those formal and thematic interconnections between Browne's two meditations. "Ping" and "pong," Professor Gombrich's binary symbols, are there all right, but they are not so distinctly heard as in that game at which we bow inevitably to the Chinese. We know the modes, the genres in this book as Don Quixote knows them, by their values schematized into accepted literary forms and habits. Like the representatives of ordinary life in *Don Quixote*, readers commonly accept the kinds as metaphors, with books as metaphors in kind. When a figure challenges our modes of dealing with fiction by *living* these metaphors, unmetaphoring them into actual chosen behavior, we are forced into realizing the uncomfortable fact that any firm view of the world, any set on it, establishes a personal myth—and, if the myth is a bit out of line with consensus, the viewer seems mad. Now Don Quixote may *be* mad, as his detractors say, but at least the myth he adopted was a social one: others recognize his literary milieu (innkeepers, dukes, a canon of Toledo) and some even join him within it, as Sancho and the Bachiller variously do.

Such as it is, the genre-system in the Renaissance offers us not a second world but an array of ways to look at the real world, offers us a special way to make of culture a *common place*. Perhaps that is one reason why *Paradise Lost*, so carefully constructed along the lines of the professional, exclusionist generic theory I tried to set up in the first lecture, manages its success. For this well-wrought epic subsumes into its scrupulous structure the primary modes of expression and thought rejected by Aristotle and his Renaissance followers, history and philosophy; in the dialogue of the two world systems in the eighth book, the visionary projection of scriptural unfolding in the eleventh and twelfth books, Milton recognizes, in professional terms, the *genus universum* of Cicero's Crassus, the whole cultural cosmos. The pastoral of the fourth book, the georgic of Adam's interviews with Raphael, in which cosmology is explained and a theogony offered, the theology of the third book, presented in dialogue—these things are not officially poetic. Those episodes which are generically sanctioned—the descent of the rebel angels into hell and the great consult of the field-commanders, each of them trailing not tribal families but whole confessions of followers; the journey of a faulty, crafty hero through a sea of space; the gigantomachy of titans against God, and the victor's triumph—all recapitulate and revise essential formulae of classical epic. The pastoral garden, the tragic structure of Book Nine, the metamorphoses of Book Ten, supply samples of other principal poetic forms. There is more, of course—invocations, psalms of thanksgiving, choral hymns, echoes of Petrarchan wooing, theological debate, formal orations, Ariostan moments, Spenserian allegory, dramatic monologue, epithalamic hymn, a narrative of creation owing its order to Genesis and its richness to Lucretius, a human banquet of sense, a farcical domestic quarrel and its reconciliation in terms of realistic romance, dreams and visions, all supplied with the requisite archaeological, anthropological, geographical, historical, and moral data proper for human education. In a very real sense, this poem *was* doctrinal to a nation, a *summa* of the topics of Christian humanism. I know this phrase is all too often invoked to cover any mixture of classical and Christian, philosophical and experiential, sacred and profane details: this time, I think I mean it exactly. Without sacrificing one tittle of his commitment to good letters, without failing to recognize any of his debts to classical and classicizing dictates of form and topic, Milton has all the same provided us with an encyclopedia running from before the creation to the timelessness promised after the Judgment, a cosmic panorama which concentrates *quand même* on the inevitable dilemmas of each human being, seen as an individual. From "that sublime art which" as he said "in Aristotle's *Poetics*, in Horace, and the Italian commentaries of Castelvetro, Tasso, Mazzoni, and others, teaches what the laws are of a true epic poem, what of a dramatic, what of a lyric, what decorum is," Milton took his form. From Sophocles through Dante and onward to his own time, he borrowed the symbolic forms by which he incorporated learning into the structure of his poem.

His way was generic, building the kinds into their dominant epic form so that this first struggle of the first human beings with their moral temptations—with themselves—could be seen against the range of human possibilities, represented in the poem as the kinds. Adam and Eve began in their pastoral garden of myth and romance, with light georgic tasks to perform; the cultivation of their garden was deepened by Raphael's cultivation of Adam's mind, until their tragic hour arrived. From that fall, they built back, via farcical quarreling, to the real georgic of life, the laboring in the field and for kind which was their creative punishment. The epic actions of great moment in the poem are displaced upon other strugglers; the hero's actions are inward, as his paradise is famously "within": Adam travels mentally through all time from creation to judgment, and through all space, to understand himself and his condition against the alternatives of total being. These alternatives, these conditions, are conveyed to us in the writer's kind, by kind: we learn from Raphael by a Christian Lucretian poem, from Michael by a providential Christian history, from the whole by a Christian epic—the poem is *made* doctrinally, the kinds of the *paideia* worked into the structure of the regulated epic poem. In this work, one is hard put to it to distinguish between genre as metaphor and genre as myth; certainly the negative, the "ablative" similes proclaim the matter and form of some poetic kinds as metaphors:

> in Ausonian land
> Men call'd him Mulciber; and how he fell
> From Heav'n they fabl'd, thrown by angry Jove
> Sheer o'er the Chrystal Battlements; from Morn
> To Noon he fell, from Noon to dewey Eve,
> A Summer's day; and with the setting Sun
> Dropt from the zenith like a falling Star,
> On Lemnos th'Aegean Isle: thus they relate
> Erring. . . .

> Not that fair field
> Of Enna, where Proserpin gath'ring flours
> Herself a fairer floure by gloomie Dis

Was gather'd, which cost Ceres all that pain
To seek her through the world; nor that sweet Grove
Of Daphne. . . .

what resounds
In Fable or Romance of Uthers Son
Begirt with British and Armoric Knights:
And all who since, Baptiz'd or Infidel
Jousted in Aspramont or Mantalban,
Damasco, Marocco, or Trebisond,
Or whom Biserta sent from Afric shore
When Charlemain with all his Peerage fell
By Fontarabbia. . . .

Ancient myth Hesiodic and Ovidian, medieval and Renaissance romance, Ariosto and Pulci are reduced here simply to negative metaphors—but with no loss of evocative power, as their deficiencies are seen fulfilled in the present poem's matter and manner. The mythic power of epic itself, of cosmogony and theogony, of tragic fall are surely evoked in their resonance, in service of this very particular and absolutely total subject, made total in all the ways given to a poet. The poem sums up its culture whole, in the language of forms that culture bequeathed; by the secure traditions of kind, we can answer the challenge offered in the poet's provocative commonplace, to measure how far "above th'Aonian mount" his flight could soar.

I should end with *Paradise Lost*, not only because of its summary powers with respect to the inclusionist and exclusionist traditions of the kinds, but also in respect to the fine work on Milton which has come from the University of California at Berkeley, to which all students are indebted. But I shall sin against courtesy, chronology, and closure, to end these discussions on another work. By choosing *King Lear* as an ultimate, I wish to look backward and forward, to Berkeley lectures past and future, to Maynard Mack's on *King Lear*, and to Lawrence Stone, next year's lecturer on Una's Gift. Maynard Mack put together many of the generic elements in *King Lear*—tragical, comical, historical, and pastoral—to illuminate the particular mastery of that play and to show *why* so many kinds were involved in its making.

I want to stress King Lear as a work of *genera mista*, a work even of the *genus universum*. If we run down a list of the *dramatis personae*, keeping in mind the characters' behavior in the play, we can see the immense variety of types cast into the one complex action—Cordelia as morality Truth and Charity ("No cause, no cause"), after her first appearance the Catastrophe of the old play; later, she is seen as romance-heroine and true Scriptural child. Her sisters are sometimes the seductive monsters of Spenserian romance, sometimes morality figures for Appetite and Greed, sometimes (Goneril with Edgar) the intriguing lovers of Jacobean court-tragedy. Kent is Good Counsel and Good Deeds, a servant faithful unto death who passes his medieval "test"; Edmund is a morality Appetite or Lust, as well as a fine Machiavel—and the presenter too from older English comedy. Childe Edgar runs through the range of English social classes from beggar to king, in the romance way, and manages also to be the presenter of a little morality-play of his own. Their father Gloucester is a bumbling *senex* as well as a Senecan victim; he learns his stoicism the hardest way. Burgundy and France exemplify false and faithful suitors out of romance and ballad: France speaks as sonnet-lovers do, on faith of love. Cornwall contrasts with his brother-in-law as an entirely lawless new man, a figure of power who reckons by the book. That he should be slain by the Nemesis-figure of a servant is justice enough—but that Shakespeare should cast a *servant* as that Justice seems extraordinary, until we remember what Jonas

Barish has taught us of the meanings of "service" in this play. The Fool we know from *sottie* and other comic forms of an earlier age; he partakes as well of the double-edged folly of Erasmus' Stultitia. Like her, he recognizes the comic in the tragic; like her, he points his finger at things as they are. As for Lear, like Gloucester, he falls from high place, his *casus* making a great rumble in the world. As *senex iratus*, he acts in the comic mode; but in spite of these comic phases, he too works in the stoic style of this play's virtue, his stoicism learnt rather from Seneca's plays than from his essays. Only after the greatest violence of spirit and denial of kind does King Lear come to his endurance.

Perhaps in the Theophrastan Oswald we see how much this play of disguise, clothing, investiture, divestiture is in fact *en travesti*: variously the characters take on other roles, speak the thing which is not, speak out of their true character, even when they have taken on highly stereotyped roles (Edgar, Kent). Just at the generic level, characters are out of character. Only the Fool ("no knave, perdy") and Oswald, at different ends of the moral spectrum, show that they are what they are, the one a true fool, the other tailor-made. And yet the genre-system works too, to secure us in the confusion it also creates and exploits: the adage-comments of Edgar and Cordelia, the archaic forms in the Gloucester-plot balance us against the buffets the main plot deals its audience. We cannot altogether blame the tasteless Tate for making Edgar and Cordelia marry at the end of his version of the play—after all, their respective romance-roles would conventionally have dictated just such an ending. It is Shakespeare's peculiar art to get things both ways—to make us honor the conventional even as we are dazzled by the unconventional. Perhaps the non-marriage of Edgar and Cordelia, the reversal of expectation in Cordelia's death, the upside-downing by the Fool even of the topos of the world-upside-down, may offer one way to appreciate what it is that Shakespeare does with the elements of his craft. Here, a silent dialogue is constantly carried on between the particular extrageneric behavior of these characters and the generic norms which they so brilliantly violate.

I want to stress the play's archaic and very modern elements—the morality-structure which we recognize in some of the symbolic actions and gestures, even whole scenes of the play; the thematic *sottie* by which characters are stripped to show their fool's nature; the archaic plot-elements of folklore choice and *rite de passage*, as against the fancy private-theater arrangements of the first scene and the emblematic tableau on the heath and in the farmhouse-trial, as well as in the modernist, revisionist paradoxes unmetaphored in the play's action.

It is by the opposition and interplay of these traditional and conventional elements that we can see how much *King Lear* is a play about precisely the contemporary social crisis Lawrence Stone has so beautifully described and analyzed in his fat book on the Renaissance aristocratic crisis in England. There we can read at length about the particular ways in which a modern centralized state attempted to control its nobility—by cutting down on armed retinues, or private armies; by encouraging the building of peaceful palaces with gardens (like, I imagine, Goneril's great house as against the fortified castles from which noblemen ruled like kings in their region or like, perhaps, the little seat of the Earl of Gloucester, which has "scarce a bush for miles around"); by encouraging courtiers to dress "gorgeously," as Goneril dresses, or Oswald.

It is no longer necessary to locate Lear's destruction in his abdication from responsibilities of kingship, as for years we have heard from Professor Tillyard and his epigoni. Abdication was by no means unheard-of in the Renaissance, as the very different examples of Charles V and Mary Stuart testify. Rather, Lear's destruction fits very well into the pattern of the historical crisis of the nobility, an alteration from the *mores* of deference to the customs of exchange. Lear backslid, in terms of his treatment of his heiresses, more by lack of human judgment than by lack of generosity: his planning to divide his goods (in this case, his kingdom) among his daughters was, after all, what many grandees did for their coheiresses; and, as far as we can tell from the play's first scene, Lear has not forced their spouses on his daughters. We can see in Goneril and Regan something of the splendor of personal adornment with which noblemen deprived of their personal arms were forced to satisfy themselves. In Gloucester's casual treatment of his bastard son we can see how automatic was what Stone called the "winner-take-all doctrine of primogeniture"—and, in Gloucester's prompt substitution of Edgar by Edmund as his heir, the pressures upon noble families to secure a male heir. The paternalistic ethos of old noblemen which Stone postulates can be seen in Gloucester's tenant's devotion as well as in Lear's attitude to his Fool ("In, boy, in"). But noblemen were, on the whole, oblivious to the plight of the kingdom's poor—only Edgar, in an amazing speech on destitution, demonstrates real imaginative awareness of the difficulties of poverty. Perhaps this insight suffices to make him a good candidate for kingship.

In Sigurd Burckhardt's brilliant paper on this play, we find some explanation of why Lear took Cordelia so seriously, as well as why he stuck so determinedly to his own word. A man's word, especially a king's word, bound in full personal integrity: neither Cordelia nor Lear could retract their statements in that first scene. Historically, however, such behavior was obsolete, for the meaning of personal honor was shifting radically in this period. With that shift came other changes as well—Gloucester, astonished at Cornwall's and Regan's breaches of hospitality, is victimized the more readily by his inability to believe what he hears and sees. So Lear is unable to believe that parentage binds absolutely, even after he has denied his paternity to one daughter; and so he is the more vulnerable to attack by the others.

Although Shakespeare does not treat of the problem an historian would find central to any study of social class, that is, finances, he gives us nonetheless the symbols for that overwhelming preoccupation. Lear, Gloucester, and Kent do not count the cost of what they do: they do it in confidence of their rights and its rightness. But Goneril, Regan, and Edmund are lightning calculators: in that stripping of Lear's retinue, we recognize the countinghouse language necessary to a class attempting to consolidate its power and to maximize ancient prerogatives. Value-systems are at stake—not only the moral values which we can hardly avoid recognizing in this play, but social values as well. With Kent, the Fool, Cordelia, Gloucester, and France, Lear stands by and for old standards of loyalty, service, and love, tendered by word and by bond. The daughters and their allies, Cornwall, Edmund, Oswald, an unnamed captain, put a new power-ethos into action. I schematize hugely, to stress how professional means, in this case the disposition of the conventions and kinds of Shakespeare's writer's repertory, could be used to lay bare a social problem we now know, after several centuries, to have had much the same shape and emphasis of Shakespeare's presentation. Among the many things that this play does, *King Lear* projects the terrible psychological tragedy of jeopardized deference.

That is, the structure of the professional system I have been arguing for is not so rigid that it cannot bear the heavy burdens of social structure in any given period—for "matching" this large, complicated problem, the playwright found in his craft the symbolic forms adaptable to its rendering. Genres may be conservative, but they *are* the craftsman's tools, by which, in addition to effecting cultural transfer, even *nova reperta* may be made. If the kinds metaphorize and mythicize their subjects, they are themselves subject to the same process, and can be used as metaphor and as myth, as in *King Lear* they are used. But the kinds are only *ideas* of form, established by custom and consensus, as Shakespeare knew—"the best in this kind are but shadows,"—adumbrations of an idea of order, shapes for content, as well as the shadows cast by solid, individual works of literature. Significant pieces of literature are worth much more than their kind, but they are what they are in part by their inevitable kind-ness.

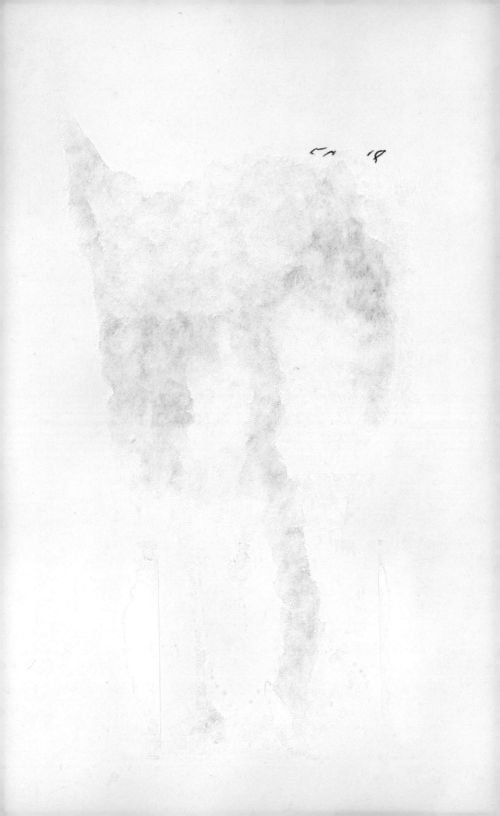